SARTRE
BY
HIMSELF

SARTRE

by
himself

A FILM
DIRECTED BY
ALEXANDRE ASTRUC   AND MICHEL CONTAT

WITH THE PARTICIPATION OF
SIMONE DE BEAUVOIR   JACQUES-LARENT BOST
ANDRE GORZ   JEAN POUILLON

TRANSLATED
BY
RICHARD SEAVER

URIZEN BOOKS • NEW YORK   1978

PHOTO CREDITS

in order of appearance: PMA; Magnum, Cartier Bresson;
Harlinque-Viollet; Lipnitzki-Violet; Keystone; AFP; AFP;
Keystone; AFP; New York Times; Jacques Robert; AFP.

ACKNOWLEDGMENTS

Quotes from *Nausea*, translated by Lloyd Alexander, copyright © 1964
by New Directions Publishing Corporation.

Quotes from *The Condemned of Altona*, translated by Sylvia and
George Leeson, copyright © 1961 by Alfred A. Knopf, Inc.

The passage on the Resistance, from *The Philosophy of Jean-Paul
Sartre*, edited and introduced by Robert Denoon Cumming, copyright
© 1965 by Random House, Inc.

Originally published by Editions Gallimard, Paris, France.
© Editions Gallimard, 1977
This translation © 1978 Urizen Books, Inc

Library of Congress Cataloging in Publication Data
Sartre, Jean Paul, 1905-
Sartre by himself.

Translation of Sartre.
"Transcript of the soundtrack of the film, with . . . minor
corrections."
1. Sartre, Jean Paul, 1905- —Interviews.   2. Authors,
French—20th   century—Biography.   I.   Astruc,
Alexandre.   II. Contat, Michel.   III. Sartre par lui-même
[Motion Picture]   IV. Title.
PQ2637.A32Z52713   848' .0' 1409 [B]   78-19019

Printed in the USA   ISBN- 0-916354-34-2(hard)
Design: Fritz Heubach   ISBN- 0-916354-35-0(soft)

A NOTE ABOUT THE TEXT

The film from which this text is taken was for the most
part shot during the months of February and March,
1972. There was a three-year hiatus in the production for
financial reasons, following which the film was completed
and edited during the fall of 1975 and the winter of 1976.
It was first shown at the Cannes Festival on May 27,
1976, in a special screening outside the regular competi-
tion. The Paris première was held on October 27, 1976.
    The text which follows is the entire transcript of the
soundtrack of the film, with only a few minor corrections
of syntax to make reading easier. The marginal notations
indicate roughly the images that relate to the corresponding text, but no effort has been made to give a shot-by-shot
breakdown of the film itself.

                                                    M. C.

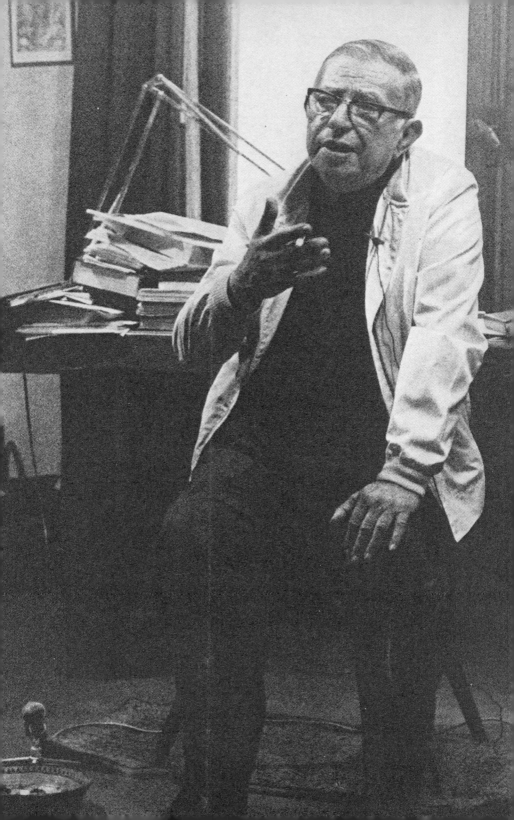

PART I

SARTRE: The bourgeoisie has always been worried about its intellectuals, as well it should. But it looks upon them with a wary eye, as though they were some strange creatures to which the bourgeoisie had somehow given birth. Which in fact it had, for most intellectuals are born into the middle class and grow up imbued with middle-class values. They come on as the guardians and custodians of that culture, and their role is to pass that culture on to the next generation. As a result, a certain number of technicians of practical knowledge have, sooner or later, played the role of watchdog, as Paul Nizan used to say. The others, having been carefully screened, remain elitist even when they profess revolutionary ideas. These latter are allowed to argue back and forth to their heart's content: they speak the bourgeois language. But ever so gently they are shaped and influenced, and at the appropriate moment all it takes is some great honor—a Nobel Prize or election to the French Academy or some other prebend—to bring them back into the fold.

And yet there are some intellectuals—and I include myself among them—who since 1968 no longer have any desire to hold a dialogue with the bourgeoisie. Actually, things aren't quite so simple: any intellectual has what might be called ideological interests, by which one means the sum total of his

3

work—if he is a writer—including his most recent. Although I have always questioned and argued against the bourgeoisie, the fact remains that my works are addressed to them, in their language, and—at least in the earliest ones—there are elitist elements which are not hard to find. For the past seventeen years I've been working on a study of Flaubert, which is not exactly of immediate interest to the working class. I have a deep commitment to the work, and by that I mean simply that I'm sixty-seven years old, and I've been working on it since I was fifty, and even before that I was thinking about it. It's Flaubert who binds me to my bourgeois readers. Through him I still am a bourgeois, and I'll remain one so long as I haven't completed the work. And yet, there is a completely different side of me that will have nothing to do with my ideological interests and through which I question myself as an intellectual in the classical sense of the term, and I understand that even though I was not brought back into the fold, I came very close to being "saved." And to the extent that I do question myself, and do refuse to be an elitist writer who takes himself seriously, it happens that I find myself involved with people who are struggling against the bourgeois dictatorship. We have the same interests and concerns.

What I am saying, therefore, is that I am a walking contradiction: I still write books for the bourgeoisie, and I feel a great affinity for the workers who want to overthrow it. It was these same workers who so frightened the bourgeoisie in 1968; and it is they who today are the victims of an even worse repression. Insofar as I am one of them now, I have to be punished. Insofar as I am writing my book on Flaubert, I'm an *enfant terrible* of the bourgeoisie, who must save me.

All of which adds up to the necessity of communicating on the government level the deep-seated

4

contradiction I feel—a contradiction that stems, quite simply, from the present situation.*

Shot of the Montparnasse Tower, still under construction. The camera moves back and we see Sartre in his apartment, seated at his desk. A number of his friends are in the room with him.

COMMENTARY: *"It was winter 1972. The President of France was a man named Pompidou. He had decided, as Napoleon III had before him, to mark his stay in office by changing the face of Paris. The symbol of his administration: the Montparnasse Tower, which at this point is still under construction.*

"The day after Sartre had addressed a group of lawyers and judges in Brussels, all of whom had come to see a star who had been indicted in France, a young Maoist worker, Pierre Overney, was assassinated just outside the gates of the Renault auto works by an armed guard.

"This was the period when French Maoists were trying to restore to the class struggle its basic character, namely violence and illegality. Sartre supported their acts as best he could, still pursuing his study of Flaubert. For the first time he had agreed to appear before the camera, in order to explain to a larger public than that which read him, the logic of his intellectual odyssey.

"A star of stage or screen who appears in public can, in the eyes of movie producers, be a fit subject for a documentary. But an intellectual who wants to explain his position is much less interesting. 'Sartre just isn't good box office,' declared those people who in 1972 determined what the public was interested in. It took four years before the film finally saw the light of day.

*Extract from a lecture, the full text of which was published under the title "Justice and State" in *Situations X.*

5

"Together with Simone de Beauvoir and several friends—Andre Gorz, Jacques-Laurent Bost, Jean Pouillon, Michel Contat, and, behind the camera, Alexandre Astruc—Sartre is speaking about his early life."

SARTRE: When I was four, maybe even three, I went to live with my grandparents, and I lived with them until I was eleven. In those days, I must have dreamed of writing, for I used to read the illustrated magazines as an antidote against a kind of emptiness I felt, a kind of boredom, which represented what I later called existence. And I also must have thought that I was entrusted by my grandfather with a mission in life, as though he had ordered me to write, which wasn't at all the case, poor fellow. . . .

READER: *"My grandfather drove me into literature through the utter care he took to turn me away from it. And anyway, the reader has already realized that I loathe my childhood and any vestiges of it that remain. I would not listen to my grandfather's voice, that recorded voice that wakes me with a start and propels me to my table, if it were not my own, if I had not, between the ages of ten and twelve, taken up myself with complete arrogance the so-called imperative mandate that I had received in utter humility*"*

SARTRE: All that represented, if you like, the shape of the writing. I had to write, but precisely what direction that writing was to take was far from clear. It really didn't matter. Above all, it was an *order* to write, a shape in search of its contents, as they used to say about Victor Hugo—not that I want to com-

*From *The Words*.

6

pare myself to him. But that is really what it was. At that period of my life, my writing was little more than a reworking of the magazine material I was reading; in other words, of little interest. Although I've lost those early papers, I must confess I'd like to find them, to see what if anything of myself I might have been able to put into them.

A photo of Anne-Marie Schweitzer, with young Jean-Paul on her knees.

But when I was ten—no, I must have been eleven, since I was still with my grandparents and a student at the lycée, the Lycée Henri-IV—something new of major importance occurred. My mother remarried, and that was a time when my life underwent a complete change, on the one hand because my mother, who up until then had been a total ally, whom I thought of more as an older sister than as my mother, introduced a new element into my life; and on the other hand, this new person became the master of my fate, and I found myself living in La Rochelle, where he had been appointed head of the naval yards there that belonged to the Delaunay-Belleville Company. So not only was there a physical change, moving from my grandparents' house to live with my mother and step-father, but also there was a wholly new family environment, one to which I did not belong, since my step-father was a man of science, an engineer. Plus the fact that the world around me—that is, a provincial town during the war—was new.

Photos of La Rochelle at the turn of the century.

As for my life with my step-father, he was a good man, really impeccable. He had made up his mind to take over the scientific end of my education. And I have to say the results were pretty sad. I remember that he tried to teach me geometry, but what happened was that I ended up forgetting the little I already knew. He used to teach me in the evening, after dinner. And then my mother—who, as I mentioned, was my best friend since childhood—became upset. She was caught between two fires. I remember one time—it was the last time I was ever slapped—my step-father asked me some question in geometry, and I don't remember exactly what I answered, but it had an edge of insolence to it, and my mother left the room in a rage and went into the kitchen. Meanwhile my step-father and I talked it out and everything had simmered back down to normal and we were back to our geometry when, lo and behold, my mother came steaming back out from the kitchen, where she'd been building up a head of anger, and whack! whack!, she slapped me twice across the face. At which point my step-father started yelling at her, and I left the room with great dignity. I mention the story simply to indicate the complexity of my family relationships at that time. And, obviously, I did take a dim view of my step-father, whom I looked upon as an intruder.

I think that one of the important aspects for me about this marriage (which was made with the best of intentions on the part of my mother: she realized that she could no longer allow my grandfather, who was getting on in years, to support her) was that it forced me mentally to break with my mother. It was, if you will, as though I didn't want to be hurt, and therefore, to avoid it, I had decided it would be better to make this break. Not that I wasn't still fond of my mother; I was, and remained so for the rest of my life, but it was no longer the same. It was something that just happened. It wasn't anything I'd worked out in my mind, not something I'd thought about consciously before it happened, nor do I think it ever had any negative effect on my mother's relations with my step-father. And I also think that I wasn't really upset or troubled by it, that is, I never said to myself: "What is all this? She's depriving me of something"; or: "So that's the way she is!" No. It was simply a break that took place between us when I was eleven. And at that point something happened. I never imagined anything sexual between them, and nor did the break come over anything having to do with sex, the reason being that they were always totally decorous in my presence, and also because I thought of my mother as a mother rather than as a woman. No, I never imagined anything, but I made the break anyway.

Filmed documents of World War I and the Russian Revolution. A cardboard poster: "I'm a provincial reject of World War I and the Russian Revolution." Class photo of the La Rochelle Lycée.

SARTRE: My class at La Rochelle was a pretty tough one, partly because La Rochelle was a port town, and the kids there often hung around ships and sailors and so forth, an atmosphere which instilled in them more than the ordinary amount of energy and violence. When years later I was teaching at Le Havre, another port town, I noted the same tendencies. And then there was the war to boot. Up until that time I'd had a pretty cozy time of it as far as the war was concerned, living snugly with my grandparents. My only contact with it, once removed as it were, was through the older kids, those from thirteen to fifteen, who were really conditioned by the war. Not that they wanted to be soldiers; no, on the contrary, they had internalized the external violence, which only came out in occasional bursts of violence or bad conduct. But those occasions certainly grew out of the war raging around them.

A photo of Sartre, age eleven.

So, if you can picture what an eleven-year-old Parisian, full of inhibitions, having lived a cozy life since the day he was born, having learned to speak a bit more elegantly than his peers—that is, more stupidly—if you can imagine what that might be, you'll realize that the result is hardly brilliant. Especially because, after I moved to La Rochelle, the kids there, in an effort to impress me, all talked about the girls or young women they knew with whom they

9

had held the wildest orgies imaginable, and so I felt I had to save my honor by inventing a girl of my own. I told my schoolmates at La Rochelle, therefore, that actually I did have a girl friend in Paris (I was eleven!) with whom I used to go to a hotel. The most surprising aspect of the story is that I picked her up after school, went looking for a hotel with her, after which we did all those things that my school chums claimed they'd been doing with their girl friends. I even went so far as to have a young woman who was working as a maid at our house write me a letter which began: "My dearest Jean-Paul . . ." and which went on I forget how, and the letter made the rounds of the school. But my closest friends soon caught on to the hoax, and I ended up confessing to two or three boys. And then my confession made the rounds of the school, after which I was looked upon as the true Parisian type; that is, the guy who lies, and who not only has an odd way of talking but also has ridiculous feelings. At that point, I was a bit of a loner. And I can still see myself walking through the Mall—that's a kind of garden in La Rochelle which also overlooks the beach—with my schoolmates in a group while I kept my distance waiting for them to invite me to come over and join them. And in the end they would, but I suspect that they took a certain pleasure in not calling me until they'd made me sweat for a while.

So that much is clear: I learned the meaning of solitude, and at the same time that of violence. And I took that violence (which was a reality for me, in that my schoolmates attacked me physically, and I responded by fighting back) and made it a part of myself, that is, I tried to feel violent myself. I internalized it in a number of ways; for example, my closest school friends were crazy about pastries, and so I began to steal change from my mother's pocketbook so as to buy some pastries for them. The purpose of these thefts was of course to please two or three of my friends whom I esteemed more highly than the others. I was in the Third Form, that is, the equivalent of a freshman or sophomore in high school, when this took place. The upshot was that it resulted in my breaking off relations with my grandfather, and this was a major blow for me, because I counted on my grandfather as an ally. My stepfather, having been scandalized by my conduct, punished me and let me know in no uncertain terms what he thought of me. Anyway, my grandfather—the epitome of honesty—was duly informed, and he too considered my conduct unconscionable. I remember that I was with him at the drug store one day and he dropped a ten-cent piece on the floor. As a well-brought up young lad, I quickly bent over to pick it up. But my grandfather pushed me aside: I didn't even have any right to touch money! And then he, with his arthritic knees, painfully bent down and picked up the coin himself. And I can tell you that when an old man of eighty-three prefers to bend down to pick up a ten-cent piece himself, that's God the Father bending down to pick up the ten-cent piece, in order to keep the sinner away: it made a deep impression on me. And that was the point at

Photo of Charles Schweitzer.

which I broke off relations with my grandfather, the second major break in my young life.

GORZ: Isn't there also the matter of ugliness that you refer to in *The Words*? You said that you became aware of that when you were about eleven, at the same time that you realized the meaning of violence.

SARTRE: That did play a part in my thinking. In fact, I'd say that it was something I was very clearly aware of at that time, though for the first eleven years of my life I was not aware of it. And I think the reason was that my grandfather played a game of calling every girl I played with "my fiancée." I remember that when I was eight I was playing with a

11

little girl whom they referred to as "my fiancée," and she didn't seem to mind. . . . Anyway, I had fiancées in every city we went to, especially in Arcachon. But when I was eleven there was a sudden realization, a further break if you will. They cut my hair short and I realized vaguely that there was something different, that I was pretty ugly. But it didn't really become clear to me until that point in my life.

My ugliness is certainly something I have to chalk up to fate, or what I might call the brutality of fate. Because: why was I born ugly? It's when you're dealing with such things that you see both contingency and brutality. That's the way things are. But I can't say that I was ever obsessed with the question of my ugliness. I mean I wasn't overly distressed by it. I used to think that was, as the saying goes, the way the ball bounces. Later on, a lot of people alluded to it when talking with me, generally with the best of intentions, but I wasn't hurt by it.

GORZ: This notion of ugliness is closely related to what you've written about both in *Nausea* and in *Being and Nothingness*, namely the element of contingency as it relates to our body, the *desacralization* of the body, as it were, with which we experience very rough, even brutal relations. . . .

SARTRE: That's quite true. In fact, I had written a book which I never finished—and never will—entitled *La Reine Albemarle ou le dernier touriste*, in which I discussed the relationship that people have with their own body. What it meant to be handsome or beautiful, or what it meant to be ugly. I don't know what ever happened to the manuscript; it simply disappeared. Anyway, later on I met a number of people, girls for instance, who thought of themselves as beautiful, whether they actually were or not. What alienation that represents, what *sacralization* and alienation! Actually, I don't think it's nec-

12

Sartre in 1945 >

essary; I don't wish people to be ugly, but one ought to be ordinary: girls who are healthy and blooming, for example, or boys who are solid and well built. Period. That's fine. But someone who thinks himself or herself handsome or beautiful has to assume a stance, an attitude of body-alienation, of the *sacralization* of the body, and what is more he or she then has a need to be noticed by others, since beauty is something others bestow on you.

Shot of a child leafing through a dictionary. He is lying on the floor of a library in a middle-class apartment.

VOICE, RECITING: *"The crowded memories and the sweet foolishness of a country childhood: I could search forever and never find them in myself. I neither scratched the earth nor looked for birds' nests in the trees, I've never picked plants nor thrown stones at birds. Books were my birds and my nests, my pets, my stable, and my companion; the library was the world, captured in a mirror; it had the world's infinite depth, variety, unpredictability. A platonist by nature, I went from knowledge to its object; I found more reality in the idea than in the thing, because it offered itself to me first of all and because it offered itself to me as a thing. It was in books that I encountered the universe: assimilated, classified, labeled, thought about, still formidable; and I mistook the chaos of my bookish experiences for the hazardous course of real events. That is where this idealism, which it has taken me thirty years to get rid of, stemmed from."**

Sartre in his apartment.

SARTRE: From childhood on, reading played a big part in my life. Words, that is books, were my refuge. In those days, my life at the La Rochelle Lycée was made up, on the one hand, of violence and isolation and, on the other hand, on weekends and days off from school, of day-long reading sessions, including works by Ponson de Terrail. It's obvious that at such times reading represented for me

*From *The Words*.

13

something like the center of reality; the rest seemed to me freaks of nature . . . hallucinations perhaps would be more appropriate. Since that other world was one in which I was unhappy, I didn't pay it much heed. It was this kind of thinking that was responsible for my idealistic bent. It stems from my conviction that reality can be learned from words, and I remained convinced for at least thirty years that a book offered you a kind of truth, a truth difficult to seize, even a metaphysical truth, and that it revealed secrets about various things. I remember that when I was seventeen or so I read Dostoevsky, and I had the distinct impression that he was offering me a secret. I wasn't quite sure what it was, but a secret nonetheless that transcended not only ordinary knowledge but also scientific knowledge, something slightly mysterious. And that kind of thinking remained with me for a long time, until finally I realized that literature was only one more human activity among many others, and as such it did not reveal any secret: what it does is no more or no less than record the full scope of how a particular period in history views the world and its people. But it took me a long time to see that. And at the time I'm referring to—when I was fifteen or so, and then later on during my last year before the baccalaureate—I was in the process of contracting what I was later to call my neurosis, that is, the notion that since reality had been given to me through books, I would make contact with reality, and offer a more profound truth about the world, if I wrote books myself. The idea was the discovery, the thing one reveals, and it certainly derived from all the elements I have just mentioned.

CONTAT: And besides, you also had dreams of glory, since at a very early age you wanted to be a great writer. But you say something that strikes me as very important, which is that these dreams of glory are really phantasms of death. In other words, you are

14

living your life as though you were already post-humous.

SARTRE: That's absolutely true. To which I would add that they were dreams of glory and phantasms of death that occurred in the works of people I was reading at the time. I mean that when you make up your mind you're going to write, at some specific moment you make contact with literature and, in fact, you assume the literary mantle of your predecessors, the literary ideology if you will, you find yourself subject to a certain number of imperatives that issue out of that literary past. You are aware of them and, in fact, they give you certain principles. For example, if you were entering the literary lists in the neighborhood of 1910, you would find certain writers, Flaubert among them, for whom literature and death were one and the same, as were immortality and death. What you have at the time, therefore, is a whole ideology in which immortality is equated with death: you are immortal, which means you live on for centuries; your body dies and you become your books. That is something I firmly believed when I first began writing. And the notion of glory to which you alluded comes from literature. You're an ordinary boy and then you decide that you want to become a notch better than you are, which doesn't imply glory. What it does imply, simply, is that at some given moment you make contact with literature and you make up your mind to write. But at that same moment you do find the notion of glory, which is inherent in the literary calling. You don't invent, nor would you be capable of inventing, literature. You first have to have had an initial contact, however vague, and only then do you move into it, and when you do it reveals to you its imperatives, its critical apparatus, a whole network of imperatives in fact, which often are contradictory, since, for example, you have nineteenth-century literature, eighteenth-

Shot of Flaubert's statue in Rouen.

15

century literature, etc.; you enter one, then the other: they are texts, texts which contradict one another. At that point you have as it were a notion of what the literature of the future should be, which is a synthesis of all these contradictions. It never is, or never is completely, but that in any case is how you conceive of it to yourself. And thus that idea of glory, which surely comes from literature. I couldn't have thought it up all by myself.

CONTAT: And what about that death-anxiety? How would you explain it from a psychoanalytical point of view?

SARTRE: I would first of all explain it by the fact that at the time I was growing up children had a religion—which was the Catholic religion, generally—and that my own family was, from the standpoint of religion, splintered to say the least. They were, to coin a phrase, borderline believers—they believed a little bit, just the time it took to listen to an organ recital at Notre-Dame or Saint-Sulpice Church, but not much more—and besides they all had their own religion: my grandfather was Protestant, my grandmother Catholic. My mother brought me up Catholic; my grandfather didn't object, but at the same time he poked fun at religion in general, although not in any heavy way. In fact, I never thought, as I was growing up, that he was really right in his views. The point is, whenever the matter of Catholicism was raised, it was something to be discussed and argued about. And then when I was eleven I lost whatever faith I might have had, or rather I came to the realization that I had lost it. When I was in La Rochelle, I remember waiting at the bus stop for two girls, classmates of mine, with whom I used to ride the bus to school, and while I was waiting I said to myself: "You know what? God doesn't exist." And that was that: faith left, and never came back. Actually, it was a full realization of something I

Shots of the Panthéon: "From a grateful country to its great men." Beethoven's Fifth. Shot of the Henri-IV Lycée, over which the subtitle: "In 1920, Sartre returns to the Henri-IV Lycée, where he renews his acquaintance with Paul Nizan."

16

had sensed earlier but never completely formulated. And so glory, and the works you leave behind you, clearly represent a worldly equivalent of immortality. In fact, people referred to it as immortality, and to great writers as "immortals," and at the same time it was tantamount to being recruited by God. I suspect that I had a latent penchant for religion—which I dare say most children of the period did too—and the need to be justified, pure and simple.

At Simone de Beauvoir's.

SARTRE: Nizan certainly had a great influence on me, because what I learned at that point in my life was modern literature. At La Rochelle I used to read, in fact I read a great deal. But what did I read? I read Claude Farrère, of course, and I read the novels that were serialized in the monthly magazines, what we refer to generally as women's novels, category novels, and then I also read all sorts of adventure novels. That's how I came across Ponson de Terrail . . . I must be one of the happy few who knows his work; oh, I know that today some of his works are being re-published, but you have to admit that a novel such as *La Juive du Château Trompette* is not exactly a household word! And Michel Zévaco, of course! In other words, a whole spectrum of popular literature, not to mention the insipid fiction consumed in those days by the middle class. Popular literature really interested me; the middle-class pap was something I felt I had to read as part of my writer's education: a writer-to-be had to read books. And at that time I had no notion that people like Paul Morand or Giraudoux even existed. And that knowledge I owe to Nizan. I suspect that my initiation into this other world gave me my first inkling of what

literature really was, what people today call literature, and yet that knowledge did not eliminate the
notion of violence I still carried within me—the fact
that I called a spade a spade. I think it's probably the
meeting of these two currents—my rough, unpolished, provincial side on the one hand, and the ex-
tremely cultivated literature typified by Giraudoux
on the other—that, thanks to Nizan's influence, later
resulted in a work such as *Nausea*. There were other
elements, of course, but those two were certainly
present.

SIMONE DE BEAUVOIR: All well and good, but how do
you explain the fact that this modern literature that
influenced Nizan to such a degree didn't exert any
real influence on you, and that you followed the
classical line? How do you explain the fact that all
the early writings of yours that I've read are written
in a classically conventional style, with mythic
overtones, and plots that are imbued neither with the
Giraudoux-like sophistication nor with the violence
you refer to?

*Shot of the garden
of the* Ecole
normale
supérierure, *rue
d'Ulm in Paris.*

SARTRE: I think the answer lies in the fact that the
hothouse environment of the *Ecole normale*, with its
stress on classical culture, did exert an undeniable
influence on me. At that time in my life I tried to read
all that was available, which presupposes therefore a
world which was no longer the unpolished world of
violence but a world of writers. And then there was,
as I have indicated, that entire classical culture
which leads you ineluctably to symbol and myth. I
refer, of course, to the culture of the *Ecole normale*.
It's a lousy culture.

Someone who did have a real influence on me,
though not directly, nothing you could discern, was
Proust. In our next to last year at the Lycée we read
Proust, at least some of us did, including Nizan and a
few others, and we used to talk about the characters
as though they were alive: "What did you say Mon-

18

sieur de Charlus has done now? You don't say! He really went and did that again!'' And on and on. Proust was without doubt an initiation for us into modern literature. I never much liked Gide, but Valéry, yes; Valéry also made his mark on us in those days. Valéry, too, speaks in symbols. There's no doubt that *Eupalinos* or *L'Ame et la danse* did exercise an influence on me. What it was was an idea more than anything else, the idea about what Valéry picked up from the beach, the pebble that was so beautifully wrought: and the question was, had it been weathered by nature or was it man's work? So far as I can tell, that wasn't where I got the idea of contingency, but in any case it did confirm for me the fact that a writer had in fact posed the problem. Actually, in Valéry's mind it had a whole other meaning, but that was how I took it.

POUILLON: Speaking of contingency, that was ultimately your initial experience, and not violence. It didn't derive from literature. And even violence came to you in a contingent way.

A hand writing this definition of contingency: "To be contingent is to be there, without rhyme or reason, necessity or justification; it is to exist without the right to exist."

At Simone de Beauvoir's apartment.

SARTRE: The first time I ever talked about contingency was in a notebook I picked up in the Paris subway one day. On its cover was written ''Midy Suppositories,'' and it was doubtless one of those notebooks given away free to doctors. Inside it was indexed alphabetically, with various pages marked A, B, C, D, etc., but nothing had been written on them. It may well have been this notebook that gave me the idea to make one of the characters in *Nausea* self-taught, someone who teaches himself alphabetically. I would record my thoughts in alphabetical order for one simple reason, and that was that the notebook was set up that way. So if I had a thought

19

about Love, for instance, I would enter it under L, and if an idea came to me about War, I'd record it under the letter W. And that way I had all sorts of ideas. . . .

It was about this time that I had the idea of freedom. I don't remember exactly where it came from, but it's certainly a notion I discussed with my school friends at La Rochelle. Anyway, I can't say for sure precisely where or when it first preoccupied me. But I do remember very clearly that I had long discussions in the schoolyard with Nizan, who was an out-and-out determinist at that time—later on he was a dialectician, which is different—and I remember that I took the defense of free will. He used to say to me: "That's a hopeless position."

CONTAT: Did you really feel it?

SARTRE: I think that I always felt it.

CONTAT: Do you remember precisely when?

SARTRE: You mean when it first had that name? I have no idea. In all likelihood, if I were pressed to pin it down, I'd say when I was in my last year at the Lycée, in which case it would have been in Paris. But I can say with certainty that I felt it before, the notion of freedom and responsibility. And it perhaps stems from the fact that I was a loner at La Rochelle; that is, rejected and wanting to fit in. All of which derives, if you like, from the opposition between my childhood, when I wanted to be a writer, and my adolescence, when I first learned about contingency, violence, the way things are. It's quite possible that that made its mark.

I also think, quite simply—and this is something I've gone into elsewhere*—that you feel free when you've had no family conflict when you were a child—as was the case with me. When you've been loved by your mother and, in short, when you've

*Especially in *L'Idiot de la famille (The Family Idiot)*.

20

created a certain world for yourself in which you become indispensable, that is, when your family treats you in such a way that you think you're indispensable to it, you consequently feel generous, and see your very existence as a blessing for the family, etc. And actually, for a long time I mistook generosity for freedom, and vice-versa.

POUILLON: You already had an ill-defined feeling of freedom when you first came in contact with violence, which means that it was very different from someone who might have experimented with violence first.

SARTRE: That's quite true.

SIMONE DE BEAUVOIR: Yes, but what about your acts of violence at *L'Ecole normale*?

SARTRE: Yes, at the *Ecole normale* we had become those who practiced violence. What's more, it continued, and I suspect that for anyone who wants to understand me, you'd have to study and ponder that line of violence, which still exists today in what I call illegality. And that obviously ought to lead me to consider to what degree violence can be either productive or moral, or consistent with a morality, or consistent with a political position. But, if you like, the just use of violence became a notion that impressed itself on me because there had been an interiorization of a violence to which I had been subjected and which, later, I had in turn used on others.

It was at the *Ecole normale* that I can really say without reservation that I was happy.

A panoramic shot, which ends on a photograph of May '68. The sound of street fighting.

Gardens of the Ecole normale. A photo of Sartre and Nizan on the roof of the Ecole normale.

At Sartre's apartment.

SIMONE DE BEAUVOIR: Maheu, Nizan, and Sartre were always inseparable. They came to very few courses because they despised the students at the Sorbonne and the classes there, while the Sorbonne

21

students used to talk about them and say how terrible they were, that they were men without heart, without soul. And of the three, they would say the worst is Sartre, because they considered him a womanizer, a drunk, and a just plain bad person. When the three of them would show up somewhere, they each turned out to be very different, socially and in their manner of dress. Nizan was always very much the dandy, with golf knickers, dressed to a tee. Maheu was the personification of the bourgeois: he had married a bourgeois girl, he always dressed with impeccable bourgeois style. As for Sartre, he wasn't dressed at all; he always showed up with an open-necked shirt, more or less clean, and wearing slippers of one kind or another, as though he were at the *Ecole normale*. People looked at him with a kind of terror. No one dared say a word to any of them, and they on the other hand refused to lower themselves to talk with anyone else. The first one I met was Maheu, at the National Library, and through him I later met Sartre. Maheu always spoke admiringly of Sartre. "He never stops thinking," he used to say to me, "he thinks from morn till night. He's really remarkable!" This, of course, intrigued me no end. It was Maheu who talked me into going out to the *Cité universitaire* to prepare for the orals of my *agrégation* exam. That was how I moved into the inner circle with the three friends.

CONTAT: Just how was Sartre different from the others?

SIMONE DE BEAUVOIR: I think that he was the dirtiest, the most poorly dressed, and I also think the ugliest. I remember seeing him once in the hallways of the Sorbonne; he was wearing an oversized hat and flirting outrageously with some student—he was always flirting with some female philosopher or other. . . .

22

SARTRE: Let's not exaggerate. . . .

SIMONE DE BEAUVOIR: . . . anyway, that day it was Miss . . . I can't remember her name, but I do remember the big hat and that he was really turning on the charm. And I laughed derisively when I saw him, as all of us who thought of ourselves as idealists used to do in those days: Merleau-Ponty, Candillac, etc.

This said, when I got to know Sartre it was very different. As soon as I set foot in the inner sanctum of the *Cité universitaire*, I saw someone who was generous with everyone, I mean really generous, who spent endless hours elaborating on difficult points of philosophy to help make them clear to others, without ever receiving anything in return. He was also very entertaining, very funny, and forever singing Offenbach and all sorts of other tunes. In other words, he was a totally different person from the one the Sorbonne students saw.

A photo of Sartre and Simone de Beauvoir when they were young.

The idea of living together came about quite naturally, since once we got to know each other we realized we had a great deal in common, and when we were both back in Paris we decided to make a life together. But we never thought of it in terms of getting married. . . .

SARTRE: Yes we did. Once, when there was a question of my leaving for Tokyo. . . .

SIMONE DE BEAUVOIR: Yes, a little later than the time I'm referring to. At that time, when Sartre wanted to go to Japan, I had other plans. Mine called for going to Budapest as I recall, and it was agreed that we would meet again two years later. I was convinced that things would work out as planned. And then he didn't leave for Japan, he was called up for his military service, and so things worked out differently, much more easily than we had anticipated, and there wasn't any separation. But there was

23

another time when we did vaguely talk about marriage. We had spent two years together in Paris, where there had never been any problem about seeing each other, and then I received an appointment as professor in Marseille. We were faced with a real separation, and Sartre very sweetly suggested that we get married, which would have meant that we both would have had the right to request teaching assignments in the same city. But personally I didn't want to get married, especially since I knew that Sartre was even less interested than I. He was already chafing at being a professor, that is, having a censor, and if on top of that he were to be married, it would have made him chafe even more! And since there was no question in my mind of having children—not that I had always thought this way; perhaps when I was eighteen or nineteen and had pictured myself as marrying some middle-class man, I had no aversion a priori to the notion of having children; but later, considering the kind of life I intended to lead, in which I had, on the one hand, to earn my living and, on the other hand, to write, there was no place in it for children.

Shots of Montparnasse in 1930: various cafés, including La Coupole, Le Dôme, and Le Sélect. At Simone de Beauvoir's.

POUILLON: Some time back you told us that it was through Nizan that you had discovered modern literature. What about surrealism? Didn't that play any role at all?
SARTRE: I knew what it was, but it really hadn't played any meaningful role.* I know for instance

*After we screened the film for Sartre for the first time, he remarked that what he had said about surrealism wasn't quite accurate and that, as *Nausea* demonstrates, there was an influence. Simone de Beauvoir's memoirs, especially *The Prime of Life*, also bear this out.

24

Sartre with André Gide in Cuverville, 1945 >

that it had an importance, but one I would term modified, since we kept it at arm's length.

POUILLON: Was the real discovery, in terms of importance to you, Husserl?

SARTRE: Yes, but much later. I entered *L'Ecole normale* in 1924, we passed our *agrégation** in 1929, and it was somewhere in the neighborhood of 1933. . . .

POUILLON: As late as that?

SARTRE: Yes, no earlier than 1933. I didn't know who Husserl was; he wasn't part of the French cultural tradition. . . .

SIMONE DE BEAUVOIR: We didn't even know who Hegel was!

SARTRE: That's right, we didn't. It was Lachelier who used to say: "There won't be any Hegel as long as I'm around!" And Brunschvig, in his *La Conscience occidentale*, devoted no more than a few pages to Hegel, and not a word about Marx!

The result, as I have often said, is that I was behind, behind in relation to all my fellow students for whom Freud, Marx, and surrealism represented experiments that they might well argue over and dispute but which they nonetheless shared to some degree, experiments which were of their own time. I was still working my way out of Claude Farrère, in a certain sense.

CONTAT: What led you to write a graduate thesis on the subject of the imagination?

SARTRE: I suppose that at that period of my life I had some ideas about the image—I refer to the time when I was at *L'Ecole normale*—and later I had the feeling that that was the first thing I ought to do. The idea that sensation was not identical to the image,

*A rigorously competitive French exam with no equivalent in either the American or British educational systems.

25

that the image was not sensation renewed. That was something I felt in myself. It is bound up with the freedom of consciousness since, when the conscious mind imagines, it disengages itself from what is real in order to look for something that isn't there or that doesn't exist. And it was this passage into the imaginary that helped me understand what freedom is. For instance, if one person asks another: "Where is your friend Pierre?" and it turns out that he's in Berlin, for example, that person will picture where his friend Pierre is. There is a disconnection of thought that cannot be explained by determinism. Determinism cannot move to the plane of the imaginary. If it's a fact, it will create a fact.

POUILLON: Actually, we've at least implicitly answered the question asked a while back: why wasn't it Freud or Marx or Breton who attracted you? And the answer is that you had your own preoccupations at the time, and none of the three served you any useful purpose in dealing with them.

SIMONE DE BEAUVOIR: I think you've hit the nail on the head.

SARTRE: There was realism, the notion of philosophizing within the context of reality. A philosophy of realism. And by realist I don't mean materialist or idealist.

POUILLON: It was already Husserl's "the things themselves . . ."

SARTRE: You're quite right; it was Husserl. That's why, when Aron said to me, "Why, we can reason about this glass of beer . . ."

SIMONE DE BEAUVOIR: It wasn't a glass of beer. It was an apricot cocktail. *(Laughter.)*

SARTRE: Well, I can tell you that knocked me out. I said to myself: "Now here at long last is a philosophy." We thought a great deal about one thing: the concrete. There was a book written by Jean Wahl called *Toward the Concrete* which gave

26

us all a lot of food for thought because, although we didn't think the concrete was what Wahl thought it was (in his case it was pluralism), we did think that it existed. . . . We all wanted to know what a table was, to talk about it philosophically, that is to try and extract an essence which wasn't the essence that the various sciences might give us. I mean, not as sociologists would study work or the physical sciences might explain matter. There was something else to be learned.

CONTAT: And what made you lean toward philosophy rather than literature?

SARTRE: Oh, that, my friend, I owe to Henri Bergson. When I started at the *Ecole normale* we had a professor who wasn't well, whose name was Colonna d'Istria. For our first writing assignment, he asked us to write about the "feeling of enduring." I say "enduring," and not "duration," in the Bergsonian sense of the term. I had read his *Essai sur les données immédiates de la conscience*, and I was bowled over. I said to myself, "Why, philosophy is absolutely terrific, you can learn the truth through it." Bear in mind that it's a book with concrete tendencies, despite appearances, in that it tries to describe concretely what goes on in the conscious mind. And I think it was that, in fact, which oriented me toward the notion of the conscious mind that I still hold today. Of course, later on there was Husserl, too. But in all likelihood that idea, the consciousness of enduring, played its part as well. I remember that the paper I wrote was a transcription of Bergson. I wasn't in the habit of transcribing people, but I said to myself: "Since he's spoken the truth, why should I tamper with it?" So I wrote a paper that was, if you like, a resumé. . . .

SIMONE DE BEAUVOIR: What grade did you get?

SARTRE: Something pretty mediocre. And that, I must say, had a certain effect on me. It was the first time. I didn't like the professor, but having witnessed the truth come down from heaven that way, in a book, I said to myself: "Now what I have to do is bring down some other truths!" Philosophy became something that interested me profoundly. I didn't rank very high in Colonna d'Istria's class—somewhere around seventh or eighth. But I did feel that that was the route I should follow. Only the year before, no, make that two years, when I was in my last year at the Lycée, I could never understand how anyone could ever become a philosopher. I was always a writer first and then a philosopher, that's the order in which it happened. Actually, there was a long period during which Simone de Beauvoir advised me against spending too much time on philosophy, saying, "If you haven't a talent for it, don't waste your time on it!" It's quite simple—starting with Bergson it became a vocation. I felt the need to do it, although I didn't have a very clear idea what the relation was between philosophy and literature. There's no doubt that *La Légende de la vérité** is a kind of essay in which I strive to find a relationship between literature and philosophy. You see, at that time philosophy had a certain literary element to it, in that it was couched in literary terms, or literary language, in my books—something I have completely changed since. I don't think that philosophy can be expressed literarily. It has to speak of the concrete, which is something else. But it has a technical language that must be used.

Shot of a shelf full of Sartre's various books.

I nonetheless consider today that philosophy is the unifying element of everything I do, that is, if you like, the only unity there can be among all the different books I've written at a given time is the philosophical unity. All my books are oriented to-

*One of Sartre's earlier philosophical essays, which for the most part remain unpublished.

ward the same center, or, if you prefer, they are all covered with the same shell, which is my philosophy at such and such a time. And since that's the case, I therefore find another kind of unity than one might find, for instance, if one were to write a novel, the whole thrust of which might be on life in the provinces, or in Paris, or novels such as those of Zola about a family during the Second Empire. No, philosophy is the unifying thread.

Photos of Berlin in the 1930s. Music. A Webern quartet.

GORZ: Where did you get the idea to go to Berlin to study Husserl?

SARTRE: Aron paved the way for me, by introducing me to Husserl's theory. Only in a very cursory fashion, I might add. At that time I read a work by Gurvitch* on the intuition of essences in Husserl's work; and I understood that it was very important. And he helped me fill out the forms and applications for my trip to Germany, since he had been at the Berlin Institute. So there I was in Berlin, reading Husserl and taking notes on what I read, but without any real knowledge of what Husserl was all about, except the smattering I had gleaned from Gurvitch. I didn't even have the vaguest notion about the concept of intentionality. So I set about reading Husserl's *Ideen*.**

POUILLON: And in what order did you read Husserl, first the *Ideen*, or did you start with *Logische Untersuchungen*?

SARTRE: *Ideen*, and nothing but *Ideen*. For me, you know, who doesn't read very fast, a year was

*Actually it was a work by Emmanuel Levinas, published in 1930: *La Théorie de l'intuition dans le phénoménologie de Husserl.*
**Edmund Husserl, *Ideen zu einer reinen Phänomenologie*, 1913.

29

just about right for reading his *Ideen*. I wrote my *Transcendance de l'Ego* in Germany, while I was at the French House there, and I wrote it actually under the direct influence of Husserl; although I must confess that in it I take an anti-Husserl position. But that's because I'm argumentative by nature. Which is to say that I'm not very smart, and the result is that it takes me far too long to understand things; I have to take them in and assimilate them completely until they become part of me. It takes me a lot longer, for instance, than it does for the Beaver here.* The Beaver is much faster than I am. I'm more like a snail. And even when I do understand, it's always with arguments and reservations, since I have to pick everything apart, cut it into little pieces, remove the bones, etc. And after all that long process had taken place, I was absolutely pro-Husserl, at least in certain areas, that is, in the realm of the intentional consciousness, for example; there he really revealed something to me, and it was at that time in Berlin when I made the discovery.

CONTAT: And you were also in those days working on the novel *Nausea*?

Photos of Berlin in 1933. One can already see the Nazi presence.

SARTRE: Yes, I was. My schedule in Berlin was to read Husserl in the morning, after which I'd set off for a walk through the city, lunching at any place that caught my fancy. Those daily walks were an adventure. And then, about five-thirty I'd come back to where I was staying, usually after all sorts of interesting incidents. . . .

POUILLON: Hitler was already in power. . . .

SARTRE: Indeed he was.

CONTAT: And how do you explain the fact that seeing Nazism triumph, under your own eyes as it were, your writing or thinking wasn't in any way affected by it? Or your daily occupations?

*A nickname for Simone de Beauvoir.

30

SARTRE: They were in a way, but only in a private way. But it didn't occur to me to turn what I was witnessing into a theory, by which I mean that I saw Nazism, as I saw the quasi-dictatorship in France, since it was the time when Doumergue . . .

POUILLON: It was February 6th, it was the leagues . . .

Shots from newsreels: crowds of Croix-de-Feu partisans marching down the Champs-Elysées.

SARTRE: Yes, and in those days I still felt that all that was an area about which one didn't write.

CONTAT: Let's talk a little about your political awareness at the time.

SARTRE: All right. In those days I'd have to say I didn't have much political awareness. What Beaver has had to say on the subject in her books is really quite accurate. I even offered her a few ideas on the subject. Anyway, we were if you like anarchists, but it was a very special kind of anarchy. We were anti-bourgeois, and we were anti-Nazi as we were anti-Croix-de-Feu.* But that was as far as we were prepared to go; and we were against these people because we saw them as people who could attack us, or hurt us, by somehow preventing us from writing. We were Communist sympathizers, without a shadow of a doubt, but we weren't members. The idea never even entered our heads.

Photos of Nizan as a militant Communist.

CONTAT: And what were your relations with Nizan at that time?

SARTRE: The best. I strongly suspect that after he had joined the Party he looked on me pretty much as a joker.

CONTAT: But didn't they try to seduce you into joining the Party?

Newsreels of July 14th, 1935, with the original sound-track.

SARTRE: No.

ANNOUNCER: *"Early this afternoon the Popular Front demonstration took place from the Bastille to*

*A French right-wing group founded by veterans of World War I.

31

the Porte de Vincennes. The demonstration was completely orderly.''

NARRATOR: *"I went with Sartre to the Bastille: there were five hundred thousand people marching, carrying the French flag, singing and shouting. The shout heard most often was: 'String up La Roque!' and 'Long Live the Popular Front!' We shared the marchers' enthusiasm, at least to a degree, but it didn't even enter our minds to sing or shout with the others, or join in the march. Such was our attitude at the time; events could arouse in us strong feelings of anger, fear, joy; but we didn't participate in the events themselves; we remained spectators.''*

SIMONE DE BEAUVOIR: We couldn't join the Communist Party. And it was just as absurd to think of joining the opposition splinter groups, such as the Trotskyites.

SARTRE: We were like a lot of people, we learned later on. Young men of twenty-five to thirty years of age would come to me and ask: "Whom do you suggest we throw in our lot with politically? And what will happen to us if we do join the Party? We don't have any experience or political preconceptions." If you have some political background or previous involvement, you can join because you have something to bargain with. Then you can say: "I've done this or that, I have this or that to my credit; I'm ready to throw in my lot with you, but if I do I want this freedom or that right." But if you have nothing of the sort, you join whichever group or party without any strings attached; therefore, in joining you have to accept the group's theories without reservation.

POUILLON: It's probable that here too, Nizan's relationship was meaningful, for if he had joined the Party in 1930 or whenever, in 1937 or 1938 he must

*From The Prime of Life, by Simone de Beauvoir.

32

have had problems. Even if he didn't talk about them, you could feel they were there.

SIMONE DE BEAUVOIR: Yes, I think he was very much taken aback by the Moscow Trials.

SARTRE: He didn't talk about them, but his wife did; in fact, she didn't mince words on the subject. But he said nothing, either pro or con. He was there. In any case, what is certain is that for us, before the war, if one talked about joining a political party, it meant a priori the Communist Party. And when all was said and done, there were just too many reasons against doing so, at least in our eyes. But from time to time we'd flirt with it. "Well, what do you say, maybe we will join." You know, it was a way of simplifying problems: we'll obey the Party's orders, do what has to be done, follow the Party line.

CONTAT: In retrospect, who do you think was politically right at the time, you or Nizan?

SARTRE: Neither one of us. Because I, on the one hand, was completely wrong—yes, it's true—not to have become more closely involved in political matters, I mean involved on a practical level, but it was difficult. . . . And as for Nizan, on the other hand, the fact is that his own personal problems brought him to the Party. I'm not saying that people don't do that; they do join political movements through other problems. But what I am saying is that Nizan didn't have time to adjust his personal problems to the Party, if you will. I can think of one thing, for example: he went to Russia with the idea of discovering whether or not, now that the Revolution had been won, people were no longer afraid of dying, whether or not death had become of secondary importance. Nizan thought that now an individual was part of the mass which was trying collectively to do something that would serve everyone, and the individual knew that those to come after him would think the same. Thus, he would see himself immersed in

Shots of socialism being built in the Soviet Union. Shot of Stalin.

33

the mass, and part of that mass would continue the collective effort. Therefore, thought Nizan, such a person should no longer think of death in the same way. So, he went to Russia, he saw Russians who still viewed death in the same way we do, and he came back disappointed. When he saw me after his return he said: "On this point, there's just no way around it: they haven't changed."

POUILLON: What were your thoughts about teaching as a profession? As a way of life?

SARTRE: As a way of life, we were revolted by it in a way. I say "in a way" because, for Nizan and me, it was *the* profession. And besides, there was art. We would write. . . . But teaching disgusted us. We used to say to each other: "O.K. We'll be teachers somewhere out in the sticks, we'll marry some hick woman. . . ."In order to bitch, we used to sketch a lyrical scenario of what our life would be. And it was only later, when we learned that some professors had actually written books, that we changed our opinion. But the truth of the matter is that we weren't happy at the idea of being teachers.

We were especially struck by what you might cite in today's language as prescribed courses or dictation exercises, by the abstract link between the professor and real life, and a whole host of other things that today are blamed on a certain type of teaching, and which in those days we only vaguely sensed. That was it. I didn't like my fellow teachers, either. I remember the first day I taught. I was in the waiting room just across from the headmaster's office. There was a ray of sunlight streaming through the window, a cold ray that gilded the floor, and I remember looking at this ray and saying

34

to myself: "I'm a teacher," and the feeling I had was very unpleasant. And the reason I felt that way was, very clearly, because I knew that teaching implied a whole area of order and discipline that was anathema to me.

SIMONE DE BEAUVOIR: From what I know, you didn't follow prescribed teaching methods at all. In fact, Bost has often given me detailed descriptions of your courses, which sound pretty open. Can you tell us how Sartre's courses were?

BOST: First of all, I want to say that we never had the impression that you were bored by teaching, and second, I want to point out that there were only seventeen students in the class I was in. Of them, five weren't interested, but twelve really were. Obviously, Sartre did most of the talking, in fact he talked his head off, but nonetheless we never felt inhibited about asking questions or interrupting; there was a sense of total freedom. Before I took Sartre's course, I had the good sense to flunk philosophy, which I had taken the first time around with Aron. And I have to say that I was almost pleased at flunking, because the next year Sartre arrived to replace Aron, and he arrived with a very good reputation. There were at least two reasons for his advance reputation, one of which was that we had heard his classes weren't boring, that he was a good guy in general and that chances were we'd have a good time in his class. But there was a second, more specific reason: the day before he had given the graduation speech at Le Havre. He had gone off and gotten roaring drunk with his students of the year before, and had ended up at the local whorehouse—you can cut this from the film if you want. And although at this time he was somewhere around thirty, it apparently was the first time in his life he'd gone to a bordello. And what was more, he had gone there in such a state that he had no memory of the

35

visit whatsoever, and when later he talked about it he would say: "I went upstairs on the back of a stalwart whore!" As for what happened afterward, he had no idea. In short, everyone liked him a lot, and as I mentioned it was a really special, absolutely wide-open course.

SARTRE: I used to let you smoke.

BOST: You did not.

SARTRE: Yes I did.

BOST: Maybe toward the end of the year you did, the last couple of months. And to give you a fair idea to what degree we were on familiar terms with Sartre, in those days puns and riddles were very much in vogue, but during recess and between classes—which by the way we didn't spend out in the schoolyard but in the classroom talking with Sartre—we used to draw riddles on the blackboard. And I remember that we always used to depict the syllable *"con"** as this short man with a comic-strip balloon coming out of his mouth, inside of which was written: "My name is Sartre." So one day Sartre waltzed into the room, took one look at the picture on the blackboard, and said: "I get it. I can see what that syllable is." And then he set about figuring out the rest of the riddle.

A photo of Sartre with his students.

SIMONE DE BEAUVOIR: You have said that when you were at *L'Ecole normale* you had serious trepidations at the prospect of becoming a teacher. And the next thing you knew you wound up as a professor at Le Havre. Is there any relationship between this annoyance on the one hand and that kind of neurosis

*Which can be both the prefix "con," as in English, or French slang meaning "jerk" or "dumb ass."

36

you suffered from during the first years you spent at Le Havre on the other?

SARTRE: I suppose there is. But it's complicated, because at the same time I was beginning to like teaching. I think it stemmed more from the fact that I was moving into the adult world. Think a little about what my life had been up till then. What had it consisted of? There were those years at *L'Ecole normale*, which I thoroughly enjoyed, and then my military service, which, while less enjoyable, nonetheless kept me part of a group. And then I was out on my own, as an individual, with you to be sure, but on the threshold of adulthood, and I think it was that passage, from the collective life of youth to the adult world, that I found so difficult and disagreeable.

SIMONE DE BEAUVOIR: Your neurosis is also certainly bound up with your experiments with mescaline, even if that doesn't explain it fully.

SARTRE: That is an incidental cause, especially since mescaline given by another doctor experimenting with the drug, gave very pleasant hallucinations—something I only learned later. But since I had been experimenting with Lâgache, who's rather saturnine and who had said to me, "What it does to you is terrible!", I ended up having all sorts of unpleasant images. My first contact with mescaline took place in a partially lighted room in which all the objects changed shape according to real perspective. I saw the hand and foot of one of the doctors who was watching me increase in size as he came toward me, and grow smaller as he moved away. What was more, there was in the visions a knowledge that transformed them in a strange way. For instance, there was an umbrella hanging on a coat rack, and I had the impression it was a vulture. The cloth part of the umbrella became the wings, and then there was a neck and a kind of beak. It was seen like that. I knew

37

Sartre during a rehearsal for
THE RESPECTABLE PROSTITUTE, *Theâtre Antoine, 1946*

Sartre and Simone de Beauvoir on the ship JUNO
travelling from Gothenborg to Stockholm

that it wasn't a vulture, but I couldn't prevent myself from seeing it as one. And when I left I had strange visions, too. I saw a man as a toad running in the street. And finally, when I got back to Rouen, I saw Beaver's shoe as a big fat fly. And when I say "the shoe was a big fat fly," you must understand that I saw it as a big fat fly, and I knew that it wasn't a big fat fly. And then later, from that time on, things began to evolve according to certain psychiatric knowledge I possessed. For example, I immediately foresaw that all this was necessarily leading me— why I can't imagine—to chronic hallucinatory psychosis. Yes, I look on that to some degree as an identity crisis resulting from my evolution into the adult world with its adult concerns. It's one thing to be one among many others, as I had been both at *L'Ecole normale* and in the service. It's quite another to be an individual, such as bourgeois society spawns, burdened with social responsibilities you never asked for, with non-intimate relationships on a social level, isolated completely yet expected to perform certain duties or functions. At that point such a person becomes alienated.

BOST: Yes, but at the same time you were writing *Nausea*, which you cared about tremendously . . .

SARTRE: I wasn't writing *Nausea* during the period I was ill. I was writing *L'Imaginaire*, and it didn't help me at all because there is one aspect of the imaginary I'm certain about, in which consciousness itself is conscious of what an image is; therefore I was forever rummaging about in my own consciousness looking for what I could see, which made my head swim and didn't help matters in the least.

So you see, in my opinion there were several elements: the incidental element, mescaline, which as a matter of fact I was taking for *L'Imaginaire*, to try and ascertain just what a hallucination was; the profound element, which was moving into adult-

Show

hood; and a secondary but nonetheless important element, which was my own psychological self-examination. I think if you're looking for the real origin of the neurosis, you have to take all three elements into account, although I agree that one can never really fully assess any little neurosis by pointing out the possible conditions from which it sprang.

Film clips of a public garden (in Rouen).

NARRATOR: *"So I was in the park just now. . . . Then I had this vision. All of a sudden, there it was, clear as day: existence had suddenly unveiled itself. It had lost the harmless look of an abstract category: it was the very paste of things, this root was kneaded into existence. Or rather the root, the park gates, the bench, the sparse grass, all that had vanished: the diversity of things, their individuality, were only an appearance, a veneer. This veneer had melted, leaving soft, monstrous masses, all in disorder—naked, in a frightful, obscene nakedness. . . .*

"If you existed, you had to exist all the way, as far as moldiness, bloatedness, obscenity were concerned. In another world, circles, bars of music keep their pure and rigid lines. But existence is a deflection. . . . We were a heap of living creatures, irritated, embarrassed at ourselves, we hadn't the slightest reason to be there, none of us, each one, confused, vaguely alarmed, felt in the way in relation to the others. In the way: it was the only relationship I could establish between these trees, these gates, these stones. . . .

De trop *"And I—soft, weak, obscene, digesting, juggling with dismal thoughts—I, too, was in the way.*

"The trees floated. Gushing toward the sky? Or rather a collapse; at any instant I expected to see the tree trunks shrivel like weary wands, crumple up, fall on the ground in a soft, folded, black heap. They did not want to exist, *only they could not help themselves. So they quietly minded their own business; the sap rose up slowly through the structure, half*

39

reluctant, and the roots sank slowly into the earth. But at each instant they seemed on the verge of leaving everything there and obliterating themselves. Tired and old, they kept on existing, against the grain, simply because they were too weak to die, because death could only come to them from the outside: strains of music alone can proudly carry their own death within themselves like an internal necessity: only they don't exist. Every existing thing is born without reason, prolongs itself out of weakness, and dies by chance. . . .

"The essential thing is contingency. I mean that one cannot define existence as necessity. To exist is simply to be there; those who exist let themselves be encountered, but you can never deduce anything from them. I believe there are people who have understood this. Only they tried to overcome this contingency by inventing a necessary, causal being. But no necessary being can explain existence: contingency is not a delusion, a probability which can be dissipated; it is the absolute, consequently, the perfect free gift. All is free, this park, this city and myself. When you realize that, it turns your heart upside down and everything begins to float. . . .

*"I sank down on the bench, stupefied, stunned by this profusion of beings without origin: everywhere blossomings, hatchings out, my ears buzzed with existence, my very flesh throbbed and opened, abandoned itself to the universal burgeoning. It was repugnant."**

At Sartre's.

CONTAT: *Nausea* describes an existential situation you actually experienced. Could you tell me

*The above text is a montage of material taken from the chapter in *Nausea* where Roquentin, in the public gardens of Bouville, discovers what existence is.

why you had to use fiction in order to express it

SARTRE: First of all because what I described in the novel is not something I actually experienced myself. For example, in the novel you see a character who does in fact possess a certain form of intuition which might fairly be called pathological, that is, nausea: he perceives what being is, and what the people around him really are. But I never experienced this nausea, properly speaking; that is, I do claim it, but in a much more philosophical way. It represented a certain conception of the world in general, which didn't give rise to any very specific intuitions like the root of a tree in a garden. One could draw the conclusion from it that it did exist, that there was a way in which a root, or a flower, or a being, or a person did exist, which was something I termed nausea: he [Roquentin] was excess, he was contingent, he couldn't infer himself from anything else, he had a certain shape that defied description since words were inadequate to encompass it. But to get this notion across to the reader, I had to garb it in a more romantic form, turn it into an adventure. Therefore, a kind of intuition, which was unclear at first and slightly disguised, became more and more visible until it finally became clear, the way a murder mystery leads you on toward the discovery of the guilty party: the guilty party is contingency, and that I explained in the several pages devoted to the objects in the garden. But that represents the formal shaping of a philosophic idea. What I'm saying is that I never experienced nausea in the way Roquentin does, which is why I needed to give it the novel form. The fact of the matter is, the idea wasn't really solid enough in my mind for me to write a philosophical tome about it; it was still fairly vague, but nonetheless I was obsessed by it.

POUILLON: On the other hand, there was in *Nausea* an intuition that you surely experienced person-

41

ally, and not at all like the root of the tree. I'm referring to the scene in the museum, in the presence of other people, or at the end of mass at Bouville when all the people leaving the church render themselves *things* by playing a role. That too is a nausea; but in relation to another person, and not in relation to an object.

SARTRE: That's right. Considering that nausea must ultimately be their experience, it is even a way of escaping from it in order to make themselves persons who exist, who are *en-soi* and *pour-soi* persons simultaneously, that is, beings who exist and are, and then assume certain rights and privileges, and become bastards. Salauds

BOST: You have said that you didn't really experience what you describe Roquentin as having gone through, and yet I remember having seen you looking at a number of objects . . . specifically, once I recall you watching some algae knocking against some big rock, and the look on your face was one I would have to describe as nauseated; and you also had that look from time to time in class, on days when things weren't going well, and your neurosis took the form of ill humor. You turned icy; it didn't last long, no more than fifteen minutes or so. He used to bite his fingernails, and every once in a while he would look at the class, and after a silence that lasted maybe forty-five seconds, he would say: "Look at that sea of faces, and not a glimmer of intelligence anywhere in sight!" That cast a pretty dark spell on the classroom. But in all fairness those moods didn't last very long.

ASTRUC: In those days, I think that you imagined that salvation was to be found in a work of art, in the imaginary, isn't that so?

SARTRE: There were two periods, if you like. At the time I was writing *Nausea*, I had already reached the

42

point where I thought that the work of art is imaginary but that it is based on a theory according to which the work is a real and metaphysical fact, concrete, a new essence that one would be giving to the world. Then, when Roquentin thinks that he's going to be saved in the end by the work of art, he screws up. He's going to go to Paris, and once there he'll do anything, it doesn't matter what, but he won't be saved. But I wrote it nonetheless by making him believe he would, because that had been the starting point, the basic idea of the enterprise. And where you are right is when you say that for me the problem was, on the contrary, to try to understand what being in the imaginary meant, that is, composing a work of art. That was a problem I dealt with in *L'Imaginaire*, but I did so because I was asked to. It was Groethuysen, a German philosopher who was living in France, who said to me: "But there's a chapter missing—on art." The chapter wasn't included in *L'Imaginaire*. So I wrote that chapter at the end of the book. And a long time afterwards I thought about the problem again. And now, in my *Flaubert*, it's the true rapport of the artist with the imaginary which is the work of art. That is one of the meanings of the book on Flaubert.

ASTRUC: In *Flaubert* there are some admirable phrases about language, for instance when you say: "Each word harks back to the basics of language." And when you talk about language, you theorize about the future, about progress, you show confidence in mankind and you say on the contrary that silence is a reactionary attitude.

SARTRE: The fact is, silence *is* reactionary in the sense that it's a refusal to communicate, the desire to be stone, to be *en-soi-pour-soi*, to be the being who is like a statue, who can't reply because silence is within him, but a silence compact and full, full of

43

stone. The man of stone does not reply. And that's
what silence is. For example a father who doesn't
reply when his children talk to him is really someone
who *poses* at being a father: a father doesn't have to
answer his children, all he has to do is express his
wishes or desires, or give his orders. That's what
silence is. And on the contrary communication
necessarily implies truth and progress as you put it.
It goes together. And it's natural to have confidence
in language; in other words, each one of us is, as
Flaubert's niece said of her uncle, what one might
call a naïf. It's natural to be taken by language, since
language is the bearer of truth. That's why people
can lie, in fact, because they consider language as
the bearer of truth.

SIMONE DE BEAUVOIR: There's a question I'd like to
ask you again: how do you think you would have
reacted if *Nausea* had been rejected over and over
again, and finally never published?

SARTRE: I don't know. Actually, it's very hard to say
what it is to be published, because I might just as
easily have been published and my book been completely neglected. That happens. In fact, we have
friends to whom it has happened. They publish
books, which nobody buys, or nobody talks about.
And that's sad, too. You may ask me why. And my
answer is that I in any case—this may not be true of
other writers, but it is certainly true of me—and
Beaver, too, write to be read. We don't write to do
people a good turn, nor do we want to reveal some
hidden truth; what we do want is to communicate
with them. Whatever value there is in our books lies
in people's response to them. For a long time we've
thought of literature as a double phenomenon, or
dualism, that is, with the author on the one hand and
the reader on the other. The two together make the
work, but the reader has to be part of the equation.

44

COMMENTATOR: *"In Madrid, there are still many civilians, although the efforts to evacuate them have gone on unabated. Members of the militia return to their posts after only a few hours rest. For more than four months we have been witnessing a people divided into two camps who are literally tearing each other to pieces. The laws of war have been abolished; the principles which had been adopted with the intent of making war more humane, of somehow making the use of force less brutal, have gone by the boards. What is more, in the realm of foreign policy, this war, which pits brother against brother, has taken on a new sense with the recognition of General Franco's regime by a number of foreign governments."*

SARTRE: I wrote the short story "The Wall" under the following circumstances: I was a professor at Laon, and Jacques Bost told me that he wanted to leave for Spain. And at that point he said to me, "Why don't you ask Nizan if there isn't some way to sneak me over the border." It was rather late in the game, and crossing the frontier was getting more and more difficult; it had to be done clandestinely. Now, the question was: should I ask Nizan or not? I suspect that Nizan, depending on how I posed the question, would either have let things drag on endlessly or would have done it with some reluctance. So should I ask Nizan or not? That is, in the final analysis was I going to ask him to help my friend Jacques Bost get to Spain so that he could kill himself, because that's what he wanted? Or should I refuse to help in any way?

As it happened, things didn't work out as I had anticipated. I did ask Nizan, who more or less refused to help, but at the time imagining the death of

Bost, my ex-student, age twenty-two, made me write "The Wall."

CONTAT: How about you? Were you ever tempted to join the International Brigades in Spain? Or didn't that ever enter your mind?

SARTRE: It never even occurred to me, except that . . .

SIMONE DE BEAUVOIR: What in the world would Sartre ever have done with a gun?

SARTRE: Except that, as I wrote in *The Age of Reason*, one does have a kind of regret that one's make-up was such that the idea of joining was out of the question. I used to think that certain people, who were more committed and as it were more physically able than I, more talented in weapon handling, had a commitment to join and go to Spain, or at least they thought they did. But I didn't feel that way about myself. I tried to explain that in *Mathieu*, in fact. I used to think that I wasn't needed, and in a way that made me feel terrible. That's more or less what led to the fact that later on Brunet says to him: "All right, go ahead and join the Communist Party." It's the notion of not being needed at the time, mostly in the name of a certain kind of conscientiousness. That was part of it. There was also the idea—in fact, that's what I said in *Mathieu*, and there's an element of truth in it: I said that men were much more complex than a commitment to the Communist Party would allow them to believe, and I said that I wanted to keep that complexity, with the idea that the day might well come when I would nonetheless join the Party. I still held to an idea that I had had when I was a child, and that was that a writer ought to busy himself with writing until he was fifty, after which you either go to Chad the way Gide did, or write your *J'accuse* à la Zola. And in the case of the former, you come home and make a pronouncement such as "Colonialism stinks!" The way I saw it, there

46

Sartre with Jean-Louis Barrault, 1946 >

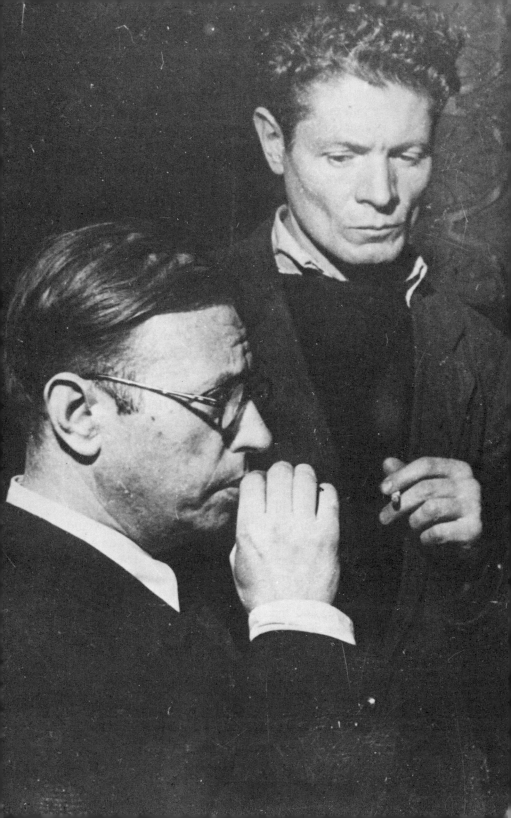

was a political *moment* to which you devoted your-self heart and soul for two or three years, and then you reverted to your former life and you wrote novels or poems. .But in the long run, there was a political commitment that a writer had to make in the course of his career.

DALADIER: *"Early this afternoon I received an invitation from the German Government to meet with Chancellor Hitler, Mr. Mussolini, and Mr. Neville Chamberlain in Munich. I have accepted this invitation."*

ANNOUNCER: *"The plane landed. Daladier emerged from the plane with visible difficulty and began to descend the stairs; he was white as a sheet. There was an enormous uproar as the waiting crowd began to shout and surge forward until they broke through the police barriers. And their shouts rang out: 'Long Live France! Long Live England! Long Live Peace!' They were carrying flags and bouquets of flowers. Daladier paused on the top step and gazed down at them incredulously. Then he turned back to Leger and muttered: 'The dumb bastards!' "**

ANNOUNCER: *"Here is the latest news. As of 5:00 P.M. today, Sunday, September 3, 1939, France is officially at war with Germany. Hitler has remained deaf to the latest French and German diplomatic overtures calling for the immediate withdrawal of*

*The last lines of *Le Sursis*, Sartre's 1945 novel, translated as *The Reprieve*.

47

German troops from Polish territory. There can be no doubt in the eyes of the world that the full responsibility for this war lies with Berlin. In Italy, Mr. Mussolini has gone on record as saying that Italy intends to remain uninvolved in a conflict with Poland. Meanwhile, on the home front, troop mobilization is taking place throughout the country in an atmosphere of peaceful resolution. . . ."*

SARTRE: I considered that war not as something absurd but as a kind of revelation, in the sense that we had lived since the end of World War I with the illusion that it was the last. That is, we thought of the social problems that arose in the twenties and thirties as so many minor upheavals, of no real consequence, since indeed we were moving toward peace, and peace was assumed as part of the total picture. And even as early as 1919 or 1920 we were rather favorably disposed toward the Germans, thinking that the fact they had lost the previous war shouldn't imply that they ought to remain bereft forever; we envisaged a Germany that in the not too distant future would be democratic. And then on the other side of the coin we blamed the reactionary policies of the French government but firmly believed that other forces would come into play which would overwhelm the forces of reaction, and thereby we would come to a political understanding. And that is why this war struck us as being so ludicrous.

POUILLON: Until 1939, you were anti-elitist, but at the same time there was a contradiction: as your anti-elitism was not generally shared, those like you

---

*Actually there is no extant transcript of the original soundtrack. We reconstituted the above on the basis of newspaper reports of the time.

48

formed a kind of counter-elite but an elite nonetheless. War, mobilization, and then your experience as a prisoner-of-war was for you an incredibly new experience, which placed you in situations and relationships you had never known before. . . .

SARTRE: That was partly the reason, I suspect—I mean that kind of need to be an elite that I still must have felt in those days—that I tended to relate to the priests in the camp. For in a bourgeois sense of the term, these priests did represent an elite, that is, they were people who dealt with men's souls, who conceived of what was happening in "soul terms" if you will, who closed ranks and had an influence even on the prisoners in the camp who didn't believe in God. So I did strike up a lot of relationships with the camp priests; in fact, they were my best friends. And at the same time—and this again falls into the category of elitism—in the beginning I was assigned to the infirmary, simply because someone who worked there requested that I be placed there, and once there I had nothing at all to do (elitism), and after that I was assigned to the artists and performers barracks, where the people whose job it was to entertain the prisoners on Sundays lived. That too was a kind of elitism. And while I was there I wrote some plays, one of which, called *Bariona*, was put on. So there's no question that I managed to figure among the camp elite. But at the same time it's safe to say that the relationships among us were not as elite to elite, but as one human being to another. It was a kind of impeccable relationship; day and night, we saw one another, we talked candidly and directly, as peers. There were, as you doubtless know, open toilets. Well, let me tell you there's nothing quite like going to the toilet in the open, surrounded by your fellow prisoners, for breaking down elitism in whatever form it may exist. There you have a beautiful example of where idealism disappears. The point I'm

Clandestine shots taken in a prisoner-of-war camp.

49

trying to make, then, is that this constant physical intimacy, with its constant communication around the clock, was a sign of the kind of communication that existed.

CONTAT: In one of her *Memoirs*, Simone de Beauvoir says that when you came back from captivity she was struck by the rigidity of your moral righteousness, that you came back from the camp with your mind made up to moralize, which when translated into practical terms meant joining the Resistance Movement.

SARTRE: Yes, that's absolutely true. There's no question that that was the beginning of my ideological commitment. But it was above all a moral position, and my ideas were naïve in the extreme. I thought that all we needed was for several of us to constitute a group whose goal would be to subvert the Nazis who were occupying our country, and that would lead to a veritable flood of resistance. And so we never imagined this resistance group—at least I didn't—as one out of a hundred, which it really was, but I saw it as something that was going to give rise to a whole nationwide resistance movement, with grass-roots support. The only thing was, things didn't turn out that way, and our group was wiped out.

POUILLON: It was when you came back from the prisoner-of-war camp that you wrote *Being and Nothingness.*

SARTRE: Yes, because during my stay in the camp I had read Heidegger—I had read him before, but it was then that I really went into his work deeply—and three times a week I used to explain to my priest friends Heidegger's philosophy. And that, plus my own personal thoughts—which actually were the continuation of *Psyche**, a work I had written some

*An unfinished, and unpublished, work.

time before but which at that point in my thinking was influenced by Heidegger—gave me more or less the elements that I needed to put into writing. And my notebooks—which were subsequently lost—were full of observations which later found their way into *Being and Nothingness*.

POUILLON: And then after that you wrote *The Flies*. Weren't you giving courses at Dullin's?*

SARTRE: Yes, I was professor of theater history. At that time Dullin was at the Sarah Bernhardt Theater, and he wanted to expand the scope of the courses he was giving. He was already giving some at the Atelier,** but he wanted to develop them even further. So he was presenting courses himself, as was Barrault,*** and several other leading theater people of the period. But he also wanted his students to have some notion of theatrical culture, so he asked me to give a course on the history of theater. And it was then that I wrote *The Flies*, which Dullin himself—I had been close to him since before the war—played in. The play was put on, without much success I might add. But still, the people who did come were for the most part young people who had a certain sense of what resistance meant, and who understood the deeper meanings of the play.

CONTAT: Today, the Far Right maintains that you put on *The Flies* during the Occupation with the

*Charles Dullin (1885-1949). A leading French actor, producer, and drama teacher of his day.
**The Théâtre de l'Atelier, which after the war and under Dullin's impetus and direction, gained a reputation as one of the outstanding experimental theaters in France.
***Jean-Louis Barrault (1910-   ), a great French actor, director, and producer, was a pupil of Dullin's.

51

blessing of the German censors. Back in 1960, Malraux himself leveled the same charge against you when he was in Brazil. What exactly is the truth on that score?

SARTRE: I can tell you that I asked permission to put on *The Flies* from various organizations, including the C.N.E., the National Committee; the C.N.R., the National Resistance Committee; the Literary Committee, and the Writers Committee, and they all said yes. I can also tell you that in the newspaper *Les Lettres Nouvelles*, run by this same group, a favorable, albeit compromising, review appeared. It very clearly revealed the message I had wanted to convey.

Shots of German troops in Paris.

PART II

SARTRE'S VOICE IN 1944: *"Never were we more free*
than under the Germans. We had lost all our rights,
first and foremost the right to speak; we were openly
insulted daily, and we had to remain silent; we were
deported en masse, because we were workers,
because we were Jews, because we were political
prisoners. Everywhere we looked—on the walls, in
the newspapers, on the movie screens—we kept se-
eing that foul and insipid image that our oppressors
wanted us to believe was the way we really were.
Because of all this we were free. Since the Nazi
poison was seeping into our very thoughts, each
accurate thought was a victory; since an all-power-
ful police was trying to coerce us into silence, each
word became as precious as a declaration of princi-
ple; since we were hunted, each gesture had the
weight of a commitment. The often frightful circum-
stances of our struggle enabled us finally to live,
undisguised and fully revealed, that awful, unbear-
able situation that we call the human condition.
Exile, captivity, and especially death, which in hap-
pier times we conceal from ourselves, were the ob-
jects of our constant concern, and we came to the
realization that they are not avoidable accidents nor
even constant threats from without: no, we saw that
they were in fact our lot, our destiny, the profound
source of our reality as men. Every second of our

55

lives we felt the full meaning of that banal little phrase: 'Man is immortal.' And every choice that each of us made was authentic, because it was made in the presence of death, because it could be expressed in the form: 'Death rather than . . .' I am not referring here to the elite among us who were active members of the Resistance Movement, but about all Frenchmen who at every hour day and night for four years said 'no.' The cruelty of the enemy drove us to the extreme limits of this situation by forcing us to ask those questions which in times of peace can be avoided. Each of us—and what Frenchman was not at some time or another during this period in this position?—who had some knowledge of the resistance operations was led to ask himself the agonizing question: 'If they torture me, will I hold out?'. Thus the very question of freedom was posed, and we were brought to the edge of the deepest knowledge that man can have about himself. For the secret of a man is not his Oedipus complex or his inferiority complex; it is the limit of his freedom, it is his ability to resist torture and death.

"Those who fought in the underground movement learned, by the very conditions of their battle, a new experience: they did not fight in the open as soldiers; they were in all circumstances alone; they were hunted alone and arrested alone. And when they were arrested, they were naked and alone to face torture. Their torturers, who were clean-shaven, well-fed and well-dressed, looked upon this wretched flesh with complete disdain, and a combination of their smug consciences and position of power made it seem as though right was on their side. And we were alone, without a single helping hand anywhere. And yet, in the depths of that solitude, others were present, all the others, all the comrades of the Resistance Movement they were defending. A word

Sartre with Francois Muriac at the CAFÉ DU PALAIS ROYAL, *discussing a demonstration for peace in Algeria,* > *that had just been forbidden by the police, 1957*

was all it took for ten or a hundred arrests. Isn't that total responsibility, the revelation of our freedom in total solitude? Thus, in shadow and blood, a republic was formed, the strongest of republics. Each citizen knew he was dependent on everyone else as he also knew that he could count only on himself; each one knew, in his complete isolation, his role and his historic responsibility. Each of them, against the oppressors, tried to be himself, freely and irremediably. By choosing himself in his freedom, he chose the truth of all. Each Frenchman had at every moment to conquer and affirm this republic—without institutions, army, or police—against Nazism. No one failed in that duty, and now we find ourselves on the edge of a new republic. Can one not harbor the hope that this republic-to-be, not of shadow but of light, will preserve in the light of day the austere virtues of the Republic of Silence and Night?"*

At Sartre's apartment.

CONTAT: Sartre, today your work consists of some thirty volumes. Does it ever happen that you take a retrospective look to try and seize what unifying thread there is throughout?

SARTRE: I have gone back to my earlier work, of course, but not so much to try and look for its unity as to re-read some passage out of a previous work. And as for the question of unity, I think there is one, but I can't say I've ever tried to look for it. I've never tried to establish it. I think that's a task for other people.

CONTAT: But what do you feel today when you consider your work taken as a whole?

*Text recorded by Sartre for the BBC shortly after the Liberation. It originally appeared in *Les Lettres francaises* on September 9, 1944, and was later reprinted in *Situations III.*

SARTRE: There are things I approve of and others I look upon with a feeling of shame. Among the latter—and I've already gone on record on this point—is what I wrote in 1945 or thereabouts to the effect that, no matter what the situation might be, one is always free. And as examples I noted that a worker is always free to join a union or not, as he is free to choose the kind of battle he wants to join, or not join. And all that strikes me as absurd today. There's no question that there is some basic change in the concept of freedom. I still remain faithful to the notion of freedom, but I can see what can modify its results in any given person.

POUILLON: But don't you think that that stems from the fact that the very idea you had of contingency has changed? When you look back, let's say for argument's sake to the time of *Being and Nothingness*, contingency was atemporal, immediate, one was there, one could have been somewhere else; whereas now, it's rather a historical contingency, which consequently implies the weight of precedents, which in turn means that freedom is not something that can be seized or dealt with immediately. . . .

SARTRE: That's it, certainly. I used to think, say during 1940-42, that in essence the awareness of being free was the very guarantee, the intuitive guarantee, of freedom. Today that still seems to me a fact that certainly implies freedom, but it's no longer completely true because true freedom cannot be seized. In effect, it is something which is an "escape" if you will, from certain conditions of history, which in some instances is given, and which as a matter of fact can be found only in relationship to these circumstances. Finally, as I've already said, you become what you are in the context of what others have made of you. And this is of prime importance because in actual fact what others have done to you or made of you does count, and you develop only from that point on. There, the personality in which freedom has been invested, what I call "personalization," actually, necessarily implies previous conditioning. Thus Flaubert is free to become Flaubert, but he didn't have all that many possibilities of becoming something else. He did have a few: he had the possibility of becoming nothing but a bourgeois, and also of becoming a mediocre doctor; and then he had the possibility of being Flaubert. Therefore, historical conditioning exists every minute of our lives. We can fight it, but that doesn't mean it isn't there. Even people who try and deny their roots and background, as many do today, are nonetheless victims of both. And that background will assert itself in the very manner by which they try and deny it.

A series of post-war articles on the vogue of existentialism.

SARTRE: In 1945, we French were suddenly discovered and translated and made famous in a certain number of countries around the world. Because of the war, for several years those countries had not been able to translate and read the literature of several countries from which they had been cut off. And it also happened because a new literature became in a way new politics. Let's say, for example, that if someone wrote a book clandestinely, while his country was occupied by the Nazis, that proved that despite everything the culture of that country had survived in one form or another. And this was the reason so much of this work was translated; also the reason why my work was so widely translated. What happened then was that I took on another dimension with respect to myself, which took me by surprise.

What I'm saying, therefore, is that it's at this

59

juncture that change occurs. There's a homogeneity between that kind of fame, which I might fairly term minor fame, that one can enjoy within the confines of one's own country, the kind of fame that accrues to you when you publish a book that is read by readers for whom you really wrote it. But then when things grow and expand and you begin to be read by people whom you didn't have in mind when you wrote the book, then you become something altogether different. What that means, really, is that there is someone else for whom I constantly have to care, someone who is capricious, moody, and very strange, whose personality traits I get a sense of every now and then. And that other being is with me; in a sense I'm double. And so I began to hear that this famous Sartre has been in contact with the United States embassy, or is working for the C.I.A. Those little gallantries are, of course, courtesy of the Communists. Or else one hears, on the contrary, that he was a Communist and was close to Stalin and Khrushchev. Gallantries emanating from the other side. In a word, I have a hard time recognizing myself in what I hear. And yet, it's in that notion . . . And then other people, more liberal than either of the above types, will say, "No, he didn't really have anything to do with Stalin or Khrushchev, but he was tempted to." Or from the other side: "He wasn't really in contact with the American embassy, but he was tempted by America." In short, you keep running into this same character, this second self. . . .

Photos of Sartre during 1945-1950.

VOICE #1: *"Esoteric philosopher, writer of Nausea, scandal-prone dramatist, third-rate demagogue: such are the stages of Mr. Jean-Paul Sartre's career."*—L'Humanité

At Sartres apartment.

GORZ: Before it was true of most other writers, you were the one whom I would term the writer of radical dispute. You raised questions in everything you wrote; in the political writings of 1947 and following, you questioned not only your own political tendencies but the tendencies of all who made up your potential public. At a time when everyone was offering some kind of salvation, you were the writer who kept saying there isn't any salvation. How did you think that this call-to-dispute, if I might call it that, and your refusal to accept easy solutions, that is salvation, would be received? And when it was greeted with hate, denunciation, and cries of "shame!" from all sides—you were, I think, the most hated man in France; in fact, you still are— what was your reaction? Did you say to yourself, "After all, it was more or less what I expected. That's what I wanted, really. And all these people can go fly a kite, I couldn't care less about their reaction!" Or conversely, did it take you somewhat by surprise?

SARTRE: To answer that fairly, I have to go back to before the war and look at the relationship I had with the reading public at the time I wrote *Nausea*. It was nonetheless an elitist relationship, a relationship among a relatively few privileged people. Whether that number was 5,000 or 10,000 I couldn't say for sure, but anyway it was what it takes to assure the modest success of a book. It was no more than that, I assure you. The newspapers wrote about it, and that was it. But those who did read the book formed their

61

own opinion, and held to it. That's one thing I did have, for in those days that was how one conceived of literature. Then, starting in 1945 or so, there was a major change due to the new means of communication that came out of the war. And since I could see more or less what was happening, I conceived of the idea of a "total public," something earlier writers had never been able to do. The writer could have a total public if he told this total public what it was thinking, though perhaps not with complete clarity.

POUILLON: That also stemmed to some degree from the situation in which France found itself in 1944 and 1945: that is, a country beaten down as a result of the Occupation, and economically at point zero. And then there was a kind of investment of literature for political ends. Whether it was conscious or not I don't know, but it did exist. And the problem as far as Sartre was concerned was that he, and others like him, failed to toe the line politically. They didn't espouse viewpoints that were in the national interest. And so people would read their writings and say, "Is that what we're going to export! My God, how sad!"

GORZ: For the entire apparatus of mediation, you were considered irretrievable. But at the same time you were simultaneously bound to and separated from the public by this same apparatus: that is, institutional go-betweens who betrayed you, who twisted everything you said and managed to turn it against you and make it come out the opposite of what you intended. Did you have any kind of practical recourse against them with the public?

SARTRE: I think there was one, and only one, actually. It worked in my favor in those days, and that was reading, reading my works. And that is indeed what happened. When people liked me, it was because they had read me; and then when they read this or that abusive article that said I was a pervert,

62

or damned, a piece of shit, whatever, they laughed because they had read the book itself and didn't believe the attacks.

CONTAT: Could you tell us a little of how you conceive of literary commitment?

SARTRE: Listen, it evolved out of the situation in which we found ourselves after the war. During the Occupation people like me—and we were legion—were involved with some party, whether Communist (as in my case) or Gaullist. And although we didn't swallow the party line hook, line, and sinker, we nonetheless felt that in the historical context there was really only one choice: fight the Nazis. There was, therefore, commitment on one specific point—a clear awareness of the value of the Communist group, a need to write about the questions that concerned us, and also if it came down to it, to defend the group with which we were allied. It was the model for the commitment which later evolved; that is, to be involved with parties of the Left, in this instance the Communist Party, and consequently to write in order to defend it and to defend yourself, to share common goals with it on one level, but not to be a Party member. Ultimately, commitment in those days was in my opinion what a left-wing intellectual could do without becoming a member of a party.

CONTAT: That holds true no doubt for political writings; but how do you conceive of commitment when purely literary writings are concerned?

SARTRE: I came to the conclusion that there were no purely literary writings.

POUILLON: Yes, the notion of commitment seems to me to be a judgment of fact as well: art for art's sake is just as committed as are political writings; there is a social significance. And that perhaps is the main difference, from the literary viewpoint, between the

63

Sartre of 1939 and the Sartre of 1945: the war and the Resistance Movement taught him that one can write a poem but that it doesn't take place in a vacuum, it has a meaning beyond its literary one. I think that's the initial turn of events. And this growing awareness later on perhaps allows you to choose one kind of commitment rather than another. But the point of departure is, I suspect, an elementary realization, good old common sense.

SARTRE: The point is, all writing is political.

CONTAT: But there are very few writers who responded to your notion of literature as commitment. It was your novels that turned the idea into flesh.

SARTRE: Yes, there is a constant effort on the part of writers to avoid the idea that literature is political.

POUILLON: Writers, even those who were close to Sartre, refused to accept the idea of commitment because while they were quite willing to commit themselves as individuals, to say ''yes, we share their ideas and goals,'' at the same time they thought of their literary pursuits as a small private chapel in which they could do whatever they pleased, with no questions asked. For that reason, the idea of commitment upset them no end.

SARTRE: Even further, we saw some writers actually join the Communist Party when they saw that it was a revolutionary party that was not going to bring about the revolution, and as a result would leave them to go about their literary affairs. That way, there was a certain justification to what they wrote, and meanwhile their literature no longer contained any political elements. They were political because they belonged to the Party, but they didn't contribute to it in any way, and nothing concrete resulted from the fact that they were members. There was nothing political about their writings. But they were Communists, that is, the man with the knife in his teeth, and therefore they were vindicated. And it wasn't just an

64

isolated few; there were lots of these uncommitted Party members. Actually, I've always preferred uncommitted literature to a committed literature of the Left. What is more, I think that you don't have to be politicized in order to be committed; that is the ultimate stage of commitment. What commitment means above all is, through a literary work, questioning or taking issue with, or even accepting a given situation. It matters little which, but it does mean, in any case, recognizing that generally speaking literature is much broader in scope than what it says. It necessarily implies a re-examination of everything. ⟶ Stop

CONTAT: How do you account for the open hostility toward you on the part of the Communists during the months following the Liberation?

SARTRE: It's quite simple. In those days, I had a certain public, a clientele if you will, and they wanted it back for themselves. Period. I don't think it was any more complicated than that. They didn't give a damn about me personally. The only thing was, there were a certain number of people who, having read *Being and Nothingness*, couldn't bring themselves to come back to the fold. Therefore they had to massacre me, after which presumably *Being and Nothingness* would quietly disappear. And on a more general level, they also thought, or feared, that I represented a third way, that is, the well-known third force that the socialists would have liked to be. And that being the case, they had to demonstrate that the third way was impossible.

GORZ: From 1941 to 1949 or 1950, you didn't envisage the possibility of becoming an intellectual with close ties to the masses. There were objective reasons for that, of course; during that period in France there were screens, or baffles, between you and the masses. But there were also subjective, that is personal, reasons. Could you tell us what they were?

65

SARTRE: Yes, because I don't think it's true to say that I didn't want to establish contact with the masses. But it was absolutely impossible, unless you were ready and willing to become a member of the Party, to be a militant Communist. And in that early postwar period, say from 1946-47 on, it became more impossible for me to join the Party than it had been in 1937, when I was completely unknown, for the simple reason that there is something called "ideological interest," which is the fact of having written books and still sticking by them. So it's quite clear that I would have had to turn my back on *Being and Nothingness*—if you doubt it think of what happened to Lukács early on—in order to join the Party. Otherwise they wouldn't have allowed me to. Or if I hadn't refuted it formally, at the very least I would have had to write a number of articles that would have been more or less tailor-made according to the Party's demands. One way or another, I would have been obliged to repudiate it. And the fact is, I had no intention of repudiating anything, and above all I did not intend to give up my basic right to free research. That's one thing that always mattered a great deal to me; I always wanted to find out things for myself. Descartes' "I am, therefore I think"— sorry, I mean "I think, therefore I am"—always has been and still remains my basic philosophical dictum. . . .

POUILLON: Thanks for the correction, but that slip you just made is nonetheless significant! *(Laughter)*

SARTRE: Yes, it is. Certainly there's a slight shift. But still, if you allow for it, "I think, therefore I am" has become a methodology for me. If you want to refer to some truth, if you want to undertake some task, be it that of a scholar, you first of all have to make sure that you are, that you think and that therefore you are. At that point, any truth can be established. But the initial truth, and it is an uncondi-

66

tional one, is established by this contact of the mind with itself. And that I have jealously refused to part with. But as soon as I joined the Communist Party, I would have had to abjure this kind of thinking. So the upshot was, I was faced with the following choice: either join the Communist Party and communicate with the masses—as a matter of fact, the question of *how* to communicate with them remains unclear; we all know how the intellectuals of the Party communicate with the masses!—or else clearly recognize and accept the various blocks that separated me from the masses, and as a result continue to work with a public that was in the main bourgeois, of middle-class means.

GORZ: So you therefore refused to commit yourself to the Communist Party by a demand for radicalism that the Party itself did not make, of radicalism within freedom, the very un-alienation, if I can coin a term, of the individual. That point is made very clearly, in fact, in *Materialism and Revolution*. There is one thing however that your foreign readers fail to understand, and that is that you posed the problem only in terms of either joining an already constituted political party or of staying where you were. In other countries, such as Italy or the United States, where there are different traditions, people might well have said, for example: "You could have done something else; there are other options." For instance, instead of conceiving of *Les Temps modernes* as a magazine aimed at intellectuals, you could have also aimed it at the masses; or, to take another example, you could also have written and produced newspapers, publications, pamphlets— the kind of thing you're doing today—that can be distributed on streetcorners and at factories. In that way, while sacrificing nothing on the intellectual front, you would have been totally consistent with your own beliefs and demands on the practical level.

SARTRE: I suppose the reason is that I didn't want to give up, in fact, the kind of theoretical research which is certainly not the prime concern of the masses.

ASTRUC: Can we take a step back for a moment? At the time when there was, nonetheless, a leftist opposition group within the Party, that is, at the time when the patriotic militia was dissolved there did exist a splinter element within the Party—however weak it may have been—opposed to Thorez.* Did you feel at that juncture that this Party would later give birth perhaps to what has today become "Leftism"?**

SARTRE: No, I felt it later on. That is, I didn't have the means; I didn't know. Merleau-Ponty*** wasn't concerned about it, because for him the question of trying to find support within the Party to overthrow Thorez was not what mattered; what did matter, on the contrary, at least in his eyes, was trying to find, somewhat further to the right, whatever elements it took to try and explain to the Communists what, in any revolution, one had to do with specific freedoms.

And at that point I realized that we had lost, for a good fifteen years, any chance of bringing off the revolution in France. It was lost by the Communists, and it was lost during those first fifteen years. And the situation today is nothing more than a development of all the seeds that were planted at a given moment. In 1944, the Communist Party was in a much better position in France, if only because today there has been an improvement on the social level.

*Maurice Thorez (1900-1964). General Secretary of the French Communist Party from 1930 to 1964.
**In the context of French politics, this term refers to the parties to the left of the Communist Party.
***Maurice Merleau-Ponty (1908-1961). A French philosopher and long-time friend of Sartre's.

And on that score, the Party dropped the ball. It said: "The revolution means work," and from that moment on it had blown it. Because while the revolution implies work, it does not mean *only* work.

Newsreels from 1948, with the original soundtrack.

ANNOUNCER: *"As the year draws to a close, the situation must be assessed as relatively gloomy, due to the problems raised since the end of the war which so far have eluded solution. And it is Europe which looms as the number one problem for the highly industrialized United States, which looks to the possibilities of modern science to equip its armed forces and augment its defense. A United States which, after Mr. Truman's victory this fall, seems ready to increase its foreign aid to Europe under the provisions of the Marshall Plan. Thus Western Europe is ever more closely allied economically to the United States, the most powerful country in the world. And at the same time this Western Europe, still bearing the open wounds of the last war, prey to strikes and social unrest brought about by the difficulties of life and the political upheavals that have periodically marked the past few years, is searching for areas of accord and common purpose through conferences and meetings between its leaders, at the same time as it tries to ward off any possible threat from without by working toward greater unity in the realm of the military.*

"Nor is Soviet Russia any less aware of the European problem. This vast land, with its 180,000,000 inhabitants, is a power in its own right, with a sphere of influence that includes Czechoslovakia, which, from having been the land of liberty so dear to Eduard Benes has become, as a result of the political events of this past year, the People's Republic

69

above: *Sartre visiting Tito, the president of Yugoslavia, 1960*

below: *Sartre, Simone de Beauvoir and a group of European writers with Nikita Krouchtchev, 1963*

ruled by Mr. Gottwald, Bulgaria, Rumania, and Hungary. And all these countries are linked, politically and economically, to Poland, which, like an amazing phoenix, arises impressively from the vast destruction brought about by the war.

"In the center of these two power constellations, and posing one of the most delicate political problems of the postwar period, lies the city of Berlin. Berlin, with its opposing municipal governments, with its divided population living according to different rules, regulations, and even different currencies; Berlin, cut off from the Western world by the Soviet blockade and living beneath the constant roar of the Allied airlift; Berlin: this coming year will determine whether or not this beleaguered city can still be the meeting ground of two self-assured, opposing civilizations."

First page of the newspaper La Gauche R.D.R., *with Sartre's article, "Hunger in the Belly, Freedom in the Heart."*

VOICE: *"Most Europeans seem already to have made up their minds who the victor will be in this struggle. We are an intermediary in a state of war between two blocs. The R.D.R.* refuses to align itself with one side out of fear of the other. The main goal of the R.D.R. is to join together revolutionary demands with the idea of freedom."*

Photo of Sartre with David Rousset at the initial meeting of the R.D.R.

SARTRE: What the R.D.R. wanted to be, in a nutshell, was a middle ground between the United States and the U.S.S.R., or it wanted France to

*Le Rassemblement democratique revolutionaire, literally The Revolutionary Democratic Party.

70

represent an area of mediation between the two. The idea was not that it should be a median line for which we would supply the definition, but rather that it would represent a constantly shifting middle ground—socially speaking—between the two blocs. And the R.D.R. was that in its early phase. But it was not long before it became what you can imagine: a certain line which opted for either one of the two great powers. And it soon became apparent that the choice was for the United States. So about this same time there was, on my part, a renewed rapprochement with the Communists, in particular over the Henri Martin affair, and then over the war in Indochina.

POUILLON: And the Korean War.

SARTRE: Yes, the Korean War, too.

ASTRUC: Is it fair to say that the Henri Martin affair, the political demonstrations against General Ridgeway,* and the arrest of Duclos** were the basic elements responsible for your radicalization?

SARTRE: Yes, it is. Plus a book. I don't mean to imply that a book played as important a role as the other elements you mentioned, but it nonetheless made a deep impression on me. It was Henri Guillemin's *Le Coup d'Etat du 2 décembre* or *Le Coup d'Etat de Louis-Napoleon*, I forget which.

POUILLON: *Le Coup d'Etat du 2 decembre.*

SARTRE: Yes, that's it. Anyway, in this book all the details of the December 2 plot are given: there are lots of extracts of letters, diaries, newspaper pieces, and magazine articles, all written by a goodly number of rightists, all of whom were for a republic, just so long as it was a rightist republic. And all these

*When General Matthew Ridgeway was appointed head of NATO, there were widespread political demonstrations in France.
**Jacques Duclos (1896-   ). A leader of the French Communist Party, Duclos succeeded Maurice Thorez as General Secretary upon the latter's death in 1964.

diaries and articles clearly reveal that, from the moment they allowed universal suffrage to be done away with, in 1849, what they really wanted was not a republic but a dictatorship. It wasn't quite clear what kind of dictatorship they wanted, although it was obvious Cavaignac's would not fill the bill; they wanted something better. But the point is, all these letters gave me an insight into just how much shit can be crammed into a middle-class heart. And at the came time I was reading that book, I was reading the adventures of Duclos and his homing pigeons.* And the two things merged in my mind, as it were, and I had the strong feeling that although the events were separated in time by a full century, they were really both indicative of the same mentality. And all these things combined to radicalize me; it was at this time that I became a fellow traveler of the Communists. Not that I was completely radicalized, though, for if I had been I would have been even further left, further left than the Party itself. But it was nonetheless a step in that direction, a start.

Newsreels of 1950. "Saint-Germain-des-Prés." Original soundtrack.

VOICE OVER: *"Are you familiar with the area known as Saint-Germain-des-Prés? A provincial section of Paris where you can, from the romantic Place de Furstemberg, look in on the studio where Delacroix turned the painting of his day upside-down. The Flore, for instance: do you think it's a simple café? No, it's a temple, with its priests and its*

---

*Duclos was arrested during the demonstrations against NATO and General Ridgeway in the spring of 1952. The police discovered in the trunk of Duclos' car two pigeons, which were meant to go into his oven for Sunday dinner, but which the police construed to be homing pigeons used to plot with the Soviets.

congregation. Their apostolate implies the renunciation of all vestiary pomp and splendor. The example comes from above, from Greco,* the original vestal of a cult whose earliest manifestations were perhaps involuntarily caused by Jean-Paul Sartre and Simone de Beauvoir, whose philosophy of existence provided its devotees with a basis for their way of life. Ah, yes, existentialism! Let us go together into its inner sanctum, the bookstore where everything having to do with existentialism is brought together in a remarkable store situated ten feet beneath the level of the sea. Here the spirit is slaked, and the body, too. From Dirty Hands *to* The Second Sex, *all the gospels are here brought together under one roof. But it is really in dance that existentialism finds its purest expression. The Club Saint-Germain, some seventy feet beneath sea level, the* cave par excellence, *where the gods gaze down, as do the rats, the thinking rats, the wheedling rats. And the African rats, the American rats. And, yes, let's be the first to admit it, just plain rats, rats, and more rats. What do you want me to tell you? That's what existentialism is!"*

A photograph of Sartre and Simone de Beauvoir with Boris Vian at the Café de Flore.

SARTRE: There is no question that we went to the Flore. We used to work there.

SIMONE DE BEAUVOIR: Did we still work in cafés after the war? Less than before, I'm sure. I say that because you moved in with your mother on the rue Bonaparte.

SARTRE: No, that was in 1946.

*Juliet Greco, a popular singer of the 1940s and 1950s, whose home base was the *Rose Rouge*, a stone's throw from Saint-Germain-des-Prés.

73

SIMONE DE BEAUVOIR: In 1946, that's right. But that's the period I'm referring to. Starting in 1946, we used to work less often in cafés.

A photo of Sartre at 42, rue Bonaparte.

SARTRE: My step-father died in 1945. So the following year I went to live with my mother, who had bought an apartment on the rue Bonaparte.

SIMONE DE BEAUVOIR: From then on, you started working at home.

SARTRE: You're right, I did.

POUILLON: What is indisputable is that you used to agree to give more lectures, in Paris or anywhere else, than you do now. . . .

SARTRE: Ah, yes, because now I feel that when you give lectures you tend to say only things that are already known. You don't really offer anything new.

CONTAT: If I remember correctly, the famous lecture entitled "Existentialism is a Humanism," which was a real event at the time in that you had to fight to get into it, didn't exactly please you. Is that correct?

SARTRE: Yes, it is. That was a lecture in which I articulated ideas that were not quite clearly formulated yet, ideas relating to the moral side of existentialism. It was after the war. O. K. It was only a lecture: even if the ideas weren't completely focused, people listened and they thought whatever they liked. Maybe they didn't fully understand, but once the lecture was over they filed out of the room and went home. The only problem was, I had a publisher who wanted the lecture to appear in printed form, "for the happy few." So I authorized the publication of the lecture for those few who hadn't been able to attend the lecture. And actually, he printed 50,000 or 100,000 copies, and even more.

CONTAT: And I take it the book sold. . . .

SARTRE: Throughout the world. And that bothered me, I have to admit. . . . That said, I'll add that there's an element of insincerity in my attitude. If I found what I said meaningful for 500 or 1,000 peo-

74

ple, why wouldn't I have found it equally meaningful for all the people who wanted to buy it? And yet
that always struck me as a serious error. There were a
lot of people who thought they understood what I
meant by reading only *Existentialism*.* Which
meant they had only a vague idea of what existential-
ism was all about. |← ⅌ℴℙ

CONTAT: In her *Mémoirs*, Simone de Beauvoir notes
that round about 1951-52 there was a change in your
life-style: you were much less carefree, you went out
much less often . . .

SIMONE DE BEAUVOIR: Yes, because he realized that
he nonetheless had to pay a little attention to this
character he mentioned the other day, which isn't
him but which nevertheless drags him along in its
wake. He began to realize that he could no longer
hang around in cafés, or do whatever he wanted, or
say what he felt like. Also, he was obliged to hire a
secretary to answer some of his letters, and sort out
who he should see and not see. In short, Sartre rather
tardily came to the realization—tardily if you com-
pare him, say, to Camus, who as soon as he became
well known created a public image for himself, began to refuse interviews by journalists or anyone else
who wanted something from him—that he could no
longer live a completely unregulated life, like a leaf
floating down the stream. He started late, but he
nonetheless did realize that things could not go on as
they had till then. No longer could he grant interviews to anyone who asked, or see anyone who
called or wrote, or reply personally to every letter.
He put a kind of order in his life. And in a certain
way, I must confess that I viewed the change as a
loss—the loss of a certain happy-go-lucky attitude
he'd always had. But it was a necessary loss.

*The title of the English version of *L'Existentialisme
est un humanisme.*

75

And the change never carried over into his psychology.

SARTRE: That was the time when the tension between Russia and the United States was at its peak, and we lived in a kind of fear that war would break out at any moment.

SIMONE DE BEAUVOIR: Yes, indeed!

SARTRE: In those days, I had the feeling, and that's one of the things that gave me pause—for I was still Enemy Number One for the Soviet writers; not long before I'd been dubbed a "hyena with a pen" by Fadeev, who later on committed suicide (not for that reason, of course!)—I had the feeling that the best I could hope for if the Russians occupied France was a concentration camp. And yet on the other hand I didn't want to go to America. . . .

SIMONE DE BEAUVOIR: Nor did you want to commit suicide!

SARTRE: That's right. I didn't want to commit suicide, though in those days there were some people who suggested I do!

SIMONE DE BEAUVOIR: I think that it was Camus' wife who used to say to you: "Sartre, it's my fond hope that you will commit suicide!"

GORZ: What I'd like to do at this time, if you agree, is try to re-establish a certain number of missing links in the chain of your development after publication of *Being and Nothingness*. How would you define that work today, or those elements of it that remain valid in your eyes?

SARTRE: I tried to offer a certain number of generalities about man's existence, without taking into account the fact that that existence is always situated historically, and that it is defined by that situation. And now I know that there are situations . . . in fact, in *The Devil and the Good Lord*, I made

76

a point of citing one such; it's the point where Heinrich can neither betray the Church which has nourished him and given him his ideology, or betray the poor for whom he feels a special attraction.

GORZ: All the same, what stands out in *Being and Nothingness*—at least for me personally—is the fact that it's the only effort up to now to try and fuse psychology and psychiatry. And what is more—and this was completely unknown up to that time, even among the German phenomenologists from whom you derived your inspiration—it is a phenomenology of the specific reality of the conscious mind. No one had undertaken that before. *Being and Nothingness* ends with a full page of questions, which leads one to believe that this work can be thought of as, let us say, so many prolegomena to every moral philosophy of possible liberation, as philosophy not being defined but rather set forth as a problem.

SARTRE: That's it. I have always thought that morality did exist. But it can only exist in concrete situations, therefore it presupposes man actually involved in a world, and one sees what happens to freedom in it. In other words, *Critique de la raison dialectique* is the sequel to *Being and Nothingness*, and morality can only come afterward. You can find it in *Flaubert*, for example.

GORZ: There is a clear hiatus between *Being and Nothingness* and *Critique*. . . .

SARTRE: Yes. A hiatus of twenty years, in fact. That also stems from the fact that when you've written a philosophical work you're drained, empty. You can't plunge right into something new. In other words, I was fresh out of ideas. And what was especially lacking was Marxism. Oh, sure, I knew what Marxism was, as I've said many times before, I had read and re-read Marx, but that is *nothing*: you really begin to understand only when you put something in context with the world. To understand

77

Marxism meant above all understanding the class struggle—and that I only understood after 1945. I talk about the subject in "Ethics", but on the level of a concept; so long as it was not felt as a concrete reality, there could be no morality in it. Therefore I stopped, because I was lacking something—some element, or knowledge.

There was a moralizing period before the war, with demystification of certain moral concepts and ideas. But not morality itself. At that period I always wanted to show—I never managed to do it, but I wrote mountains of material on the subject, which I never published—that no matter what we do, we do it within some moral frame of reference. It's amusing to make the demonstration using *L'Humanité* as an example, I might add . . .

Anyway, the idea was a kind of moralism. And from the time I became more involved politically, this moralism began to yield to a realism, if you like. In other words, it began to give way to the political realism of certain Communists or of a great number of Communists: all right, you do it because it works, and you check it out, you evaluate it according to its efficacity rather than some vague notions having to do with morality, which would only slow things up. But as you can well imagine, that whole idea didn't sit too well with me, it upset me no end, despite the fact that—ignoring my own better judgment—I carried it through and finally arrived at a pure realism: what's real is true, and what's true is real. And when I had reached that point, what it meant was that I had blocked out all ideas of morality. This did not mean that we went so far into realism as to espouse ideas such as those the French collaborationists resorted to, such as: "O.K. Hitler has won. Now let's throw in our lot with him." And that lasted till about 1965, but it really came to a point in 1968 when once again I found people around me who went on the assump-

78

tion that morality and politics are not mutually exclusive, and who were ready to fight for what they believed.

ASTRUC: Yes, and that reminds me of a point, Sartre, I wanted to bring up, something I was especially struck by. In the preface you wrote to Michèle Manceau's *Les Maos en France*, you emphasized the moral aspect of the Maoists.

SARTRE: That's true.

ASTRUC: And that's something I've noted from personal experience. I find that it's quite significant that the existentialists, who have always been more or less concerned with the notion of morality through that of freedom, after 1968 for the most part almost always joined forces with the Maoists . . .

SARTRE: . . . rather than with the Trotskyites, for example. That is why I find myself involved with people I used to know. And at the same time it proves a point—and this applies not only to the French Maoists but also to those from whom they take their inspiration, namely the Chinese—it proves in fact that when you get involved in politics, you shouldn't consider that morality is a simple superstructure, but rather that it exists at the very level of what is called infrastructure. And that is something I've always believed. In other words, work presupposes, within the context of what you do, a morality. For example, the act of taking a tool and using it implies a certain vision of the world and, as a result, a basic morality from the word go. With the division of labor, etc., this morality becomes increasingly important. During the time we were linked to the Communists, this idea was systematically suppressed, because they didn't think that way, though later they came around to it, or rather back to it. I can remember that after Stalin's death many people were trying very hard to moralize about Marxism, and they weren't very successful because it was pretty hard to find much in

79

Marxism to moralize about. Actually, Marxism presupposes a morality, but it is implicit rather than explicit. It's Mao who clarified it and gave it flesh. Obviously, it can only exist with a certain spontaneity, which is not synonymous with what is referred to as spontaneism.

So my life is made up of three distinct periods: a period of morality, whose roots go back to my childhood; realism, which evolved out of the war more than anything else, and which lasted until 1965 . . .

POUILLON: Oh, I wouldn't say it lasted until 1965. Are you forgetting your reaction to the Hungarian Revolution in 1956?

SARTRE: You're right, that was a moral reaction. But you must remember that it was also a political one, since it was clarifying a political situation, or position.

POUILLON: Today morality is political as well!

SARTRE: I couldn't agree with you more. And that is really the crux of the matter, as far as I'm concerned: whether one chooses politics or morality, or whether politics and morality are not actually one and the same. And at this stage of my life I've come back to a point of departure, although much enriched if you will, by putting morality on the level of the masses. And the fact is, there is no mass action which is not both political and moral. For instance, the movement on the part of so many people to improve prison conditions today is really a moral issue, namely by asking why it is that prisoners, who under the law are supposed to be locked up, deprived of their freedom, should have further punishment meted out to them, whether in the form of beatings, straight-jackets, or whatever? And that is nothing other than a moral stance. Not to say that it isn't political and economic as well, for as you know, prisoners are horribly exploited; they aren't paid for their work the

80

way people on the outside performing the same tasks are.

At this time in history, and I think it's occurring more or less around the world, morality is very much in people's minds; moral questions that are nothing other than political questions. And it's in this area that I find myself in total agreement with the Maoists.

POUILLON: And that is why you haven't written the "Ethics" you indicated was forthcoming at the end of *Being and Nothingness*. At the time you wrote that work, you couldn't say what you can say today. All you had was the demystification of the superstructure of morality, without having the possibility of the other.

SARTRE: That's quite true. And now I could write an "Ethics". Actually, I have a lot of notes on it. I don't know now whether I'll write it, because I first have to finish my *Flaubert*, but the notes do exist, and I may well write it. I have, when you think about it, written two "Ethics": the first between 1945-47, completely mystified—the "Ethics" I thought I could write after I had finished *Being and Nothingness*. The notes I had on that first version I've relegated to the bottom drawer. And then notes that date from 1965 or thereabouts, on another "Ethics," which related to the problem of realism as well as that of morality. I could have written a book using those notes as a basis, but I just haven't done it as yet.

Newsreels of the Algerian war, with the original soundtrack.

COMMENTATOR: *"In Algiers, a massive operation took place yesterday, after secret preparations, in which the old Arab section, the Casbah, was surrounded and sealed off by 7,000 men. While*

81

helicopters provided air cover, the many streets and alleys of the Arab city were inspected on a house-by-house basis. Large stockpiles of weapons were seized. A major underground printer was discovered. And more than 500 suspects were arrested, including several terrorist leaders. Algiers breathes easier.

"These military operations do not mean that the peaceful and humanitarian aspects of the country's past have in any way been interrupted: sixteen miles from Algiers, the Rivet Sanitarium still houses its 300 patients, 95 per cent of whom are destitute Muslims.

"The civilized world cannot help but contrast the murderous acts of the terrorist rebels with the attitude of these dedicated men and women who, unnoticed and unrewarded, go quietly about their humanitarian duties, thanks to which thousands of Algerians owe their lives.

"In the region of Turenne, an area of recent terrorist attacks, a major military operation was carried out in the course of the day, covering several towns and villages suspected of harboring rebels. Several dozen suspects were arrested, eighteen of whom are still being held, among whom there well may be the arsonists and assassins of recent date.

"The Parachute Corps, ready and willing to give its all to defend the countless charitable and humanitarian institutions scattered throughout the country, the result of a century and a quarter's worth of effort by the French in Algeria, are celebrating Red Beret Day. Frenchmen everywhere who celebrate this day should remember the debt of gratitude we all owe this elite group—despite all the attacks and defamations which have recently been directed against it. By honoring the Red Berets, you will show that you still believe in these two simple words: 'Honor and Country.' "

82

SARTRE: We denounced torture, being fully aware that torture had become an integral part of that war. And to denounce torture meant that we were denouncing the war itself. And then more specific things happened, such as the Jeanson trial, and the "Manifesto of the 121."

CONTAT: That was important for you, wasn't it? You felt that that Manifesto did have an impact?

SARTRE: Yes, but you know that I wasn't solely responsible for it. Now I can admit it. People came to me with the Manifesto already written and said, "Will you sign this?" And I read it and said, "Of course I will." But I didn't write it; other people did. Later on we all declared that we had written it. . . .

POUILLON: That's a beautiful example of the unpredictability of what one does. I remember very well the full evolution of events involving the Manifesto, how I would go up to the people and ask them to sign, and explain to them: "It's just one more petition, which will probably go unnoticed." If the government hadn't decided to make an issue out of . . .

SARTRE: Yes, that was Debré's* doing. . . .

POUILLON: There's another aspect I find strange about that Manifesto. It was drawn up in July and August, 1960, and made public early in September. You were in Brazil, I remember. Anyway, the people who refused to sign it—and a number of them with whom I had been in direct contact or in correspondence did refuse—usually balked for this reason. The Manifesto ended with two specific points: 1) a call to insubordination, and 2) help for the National Liberation Front. And most of the people who wouldn't sign would say to me: "For number one, the insubordination, O.K. But that second

*Michel Debré, former Prime Minister and conservative politician.

83

point about helping the National Liberation Front poses a whole other problem.'' And when the Manifesto was made public, no one attacked us on the question of help to the Algerian National Liberation Front.

SARTRE: Yes, that's true.

POUILLON: And at that point I felt like going back to all those letters of refusal and writing to the people, saying: ''O.K. since you had no qualms about number one, the call to insubordination, which is the focus of the government's attack on us now, how about signing now?''

SARTRE: Several of the signers were indicted. And when Simone de Beauvoir and I returned to France, we asked to be indicted, but we never were. But as a result, all the other impending trials were abandoned.

CONTAT: Can we back up a few years, to 1958, when De Gaulle came to power.

SARTRE: Actually, that was something I more or less predicted. I could see that the democratic process was rotting and that something had to happen soon: in my opinion, it would be fascism, dictatorship. It didn't turn out to be fascism, but I thought it would. What it was, though, was the downfall of France.

DE GAULLE: *"Have I ever made any attempt to undermine or abrogate the basic precepts of freedom? No. I reaffirmed them. Have I for one second made any such attempt? Why do you think that a sixty-seven-year-old man should have any desire whatsoever to become a dictator?"*

84

At Sartre's apartment.

SARTRE: Any man who assumes power as a result of a conspiracy cannot be considered honorable. He cannot be considered a valid politician. It was on this score that I attacked De Gaulle, and I did so violently because he had in fact come to power as a result of a conspiracy. And the referendums which followed, which reminded me of Napoleon III's plebiscites, did not affect the basic precept one iota.

The result is, we're still living under a government which came to power by force and had itself confirmed by referendums—we all know that referendums are always favorable. At the time of the liberal Empire, the last referendum was favorable to Napoleon III, which meant that in 1869 he still held power quite legitimately, and it was the war that overthrew him.

Successive shots of the past three French presidents—De Gaulle, Pompidou, Giscard d'Estaing.

What I'm saying, therefore, is that generally speaking I consider De Gaulle an evil person in history. I find my feelings confirmed by the fact that today we're living in an abominable society, which is headed by a band of thieves and cutthroats, a society whose origins are "Gaullist" after De Gaulle. Everywhere you look, France is currently not only disfigured, to borrow a term popular on television, but ruined, destroyed. It's a country which, after all the political in-fighting is over, will no longer resemble what it once was.

A pan shot of the towers of the new Seine river-front. Strident music.

Today, France is a society which can only save itself from what it has become through a revolution.

Close-up of a tape recorder. The camera moves back to reveal the orchestra of an empty theater. The houselights go out one by one. The final monologue from The Condemned of Altona. *The role of Frantz von Gerlach is played by Serge Reggiani, and it is his voice we hear.*

FRANTZ'S VOICE: *"Centuries of the future, here is my century, solitary and deformed—the accused. My client is tearing himself open with his own hands. What you take for white lymph is blood. There are no red corpuscles, for the accused is dying of hunger. But I will tell you the secret of these multiple*

85

*incisions. The century might have been a good one
had not man been watched from time immemorial by
the cruel enemy who had sworn to destroy him, that
hairless, evil, flesh-eating beast—man himself. One
and one make one—there's our mystery. The beast
was hiding, and suddenly we surprised his look deep
in the eyes of our neighbors. So we struck. Legiti-
mate self-defense. I surprised the beast. I struck. A
man fell, and in his dying eyes I saw the beast still
living—myself. One and one make one—what a
misunderstanding! Where does it come from, this
rancid, dead taste in my mouth? From man? From
the beast? From myself? It is the taste of the century.
Happy centuries, you who do not know our hatreds,
how could you understand the atrocious power of
our fatal loves? Love. Hatred. One and one . . .
Acquit us! My client was the first to know shame. He
knows he is naked. Beautiful children, you who are
born of us, our pain has brought you forth. This
century is a woman in labor. Will you condemn your
mother? Eh? Answer! (Pause.) The thirtieth century
no longer replies. Perhaps there will be no more
centuries after ours. Perhaps a bomb will blow out
all the lights. Everything will be dead—eyes,
judges, time. Night. Oh, tribunal of the night—you
who were, who will be, and who are—I have been! I
have been! I, Frantz von Gerlach, here in this room,
have taken the century upon my shoulders and have
said: 'I will answer for it. This day and forever.'
What did you say?''*

*Sartre, in a theater
bar with Serge
Reggiani, Marie
Olivier, and
François Périer.*

SARTRE: That play was one where I had the least
trouble finding my subject. I suspect that for a long
time I had known that that was what I wanted to write
about: I wanted to denounce torture. All right: Reggiani—that is, Frantz—had tortured. And then a

86

curious thing happened. He appears as the only character who is responsible. They are all dogs, but he *knows* he's a dog. As a result, he pays for them all, and in a way he becomes a positive character.
ASTRUC: In your theater, isn't there a certain dialectic, or Hegelian concept at its core?
SARTRE: There is, and it's a notion I still hold to today. When Hegel speaks of Greek or Roman theater, he shows people all of whom have what he refers to as "pathos," which as you know is not only a feeling but a feeling which at the same time is a right. For instance, Antigone has a right, as does Creon. And then the two rights meet head-on, and according to Hegel, tragedy results. Well, in my view, that's a notion that's still valid, that I still firmly believe. . . . But in today's theater, this problem of pathos no longer exists. Today's playwrights are onto something else. But the notion of pathos presupposes two opposing lawyers, arguing until their last breath, because there is no solution. They represent two rights in conflict. And aside from death, the only other possible solution is for one to make the other his slave. In my view, that's theater.

Photos from The Condemned of Altona *and* The Devil and the Good Lord.

The cover of Sartre's book, The Words.

At Sartre's apartment.

SARTRE: Most of *The Words* was written in 1953. It was the time of introspection, of self-analysis. But to understand that book one ought to have an idea of the circumstances surrounding its composition. Between 1950 and 1952 the tension between the U.S.A. and Russia was at its height. The anti-Ridgeway demonstrations in France and their repercussions had a profound effect on me, reawakening my interest in Marxism, instilling in me a sense of the class struggle which I still retain to this day. All of this tended to align me with the Communists, turn

87

me into a fellow traveler. At that time of my life, all sorts of changes were taking place, and in particular I came to the realization that ever since I had first begun to write I had been living in a real neurosis—longer, actually, from the time I was nine till I was fifty. My neurosis—which wasn't all that different from the one Flaubert suffered in his day—was basically that I firmly believed that nothing was more beautiful than writing, nothing greater, that to write was to create lasting works, and that the writer's life ought to be understood through his work. And then, in 1953, I came to the realization that that was a completely bourgeois viewpoint, that there was a great deal more to life than writing. All of which meant that I had to rethink the value I placed on the written word, which I now felt was on a whole other level than where I had previously placed it. From that point of view, I was, somewhere around 1953-54, cured almost immediately of my neurosis. And at that point I felt a strong urge to understand that neurosis to try and find out what could have made a nine-year-old boy slip into that "neurosis of literature," whereas other boys my age were normal. And so I wrote *The Words* and later a sequel which will never be published. Both these works represent an effort on my part to understand my life up to that point. It was in that context that I wrote that autobiography, which, I might add, interests me less today . . . I mean the problem interests me less. What does interest me more is the autobiography such as it's being presented in this film, that is to say, the trajectory of an intellectual from the day he was born in 1905 up to the present. And, more significantly, the trajectory of *one* intellectual.

BOST: When you wrote *The Words*, you nonetheless—how shall I phrase this?—tried to formulate it in the most elegant prose possible, in order to make

88

it—and I detest the term—"a work of art." Or, let's say, a compelling book, one that . . .

SARTRE: That's true, because I wanted the book to be provocative. I wanted to make it a farewell to literature, and one that would be well written. In other words, what I was looking for was that people who might read it would be led to question literature through literature itself. So I wrote it that way. But there were other writings of the same period roughly, such as "Communists and Peace," that were not written in that style. But for *The Words*, I wanted to write it the way I did.

ASTRUC: And it was following publication of that book, or at least during the same period, that you were awarded the Nobel Prize.

SARTRE: That's right. It was two years after publication, as I remember. It's a familiar refrain: people thought of that work as an indication of my political disengagement—a gross error of judgment on their part, since it meant something quite different—and since I was disengaged, bourgeois society was willing to forgive and forget, close its eyes to my past errors. It took that book as a confession, and so it bestowed on me the Goncourt Prize, and then the Nobel. It pardoned me and it thought that now I was worthy of the Nobel, an idea that struck me as monstrous. And the word "pardoned" was actually pronounced, or at least "will not be taken into account." There was an article in *Le Figaro* that said: "It looks as though M. Sartre will be awarded the Nobel Prize. His past will not be taken into account because of *The Words*. . . ." That's the way they always work, in fact: there's always one book that the Committee takes to be the author's final word, or last gasp, after which they kill him with the Nobel Prize, and then it's all over. Actually, most of the Nobel Prize winners for literature didn't last very long after they won it. François Mauriac was the

89

Sartre helps distribute copies of LA CAUSE DU PEUPLE, *one of the far-left newspapers to which he lent his name as "responsible editor", in order to help publicize police measures against radical publications, 1971*

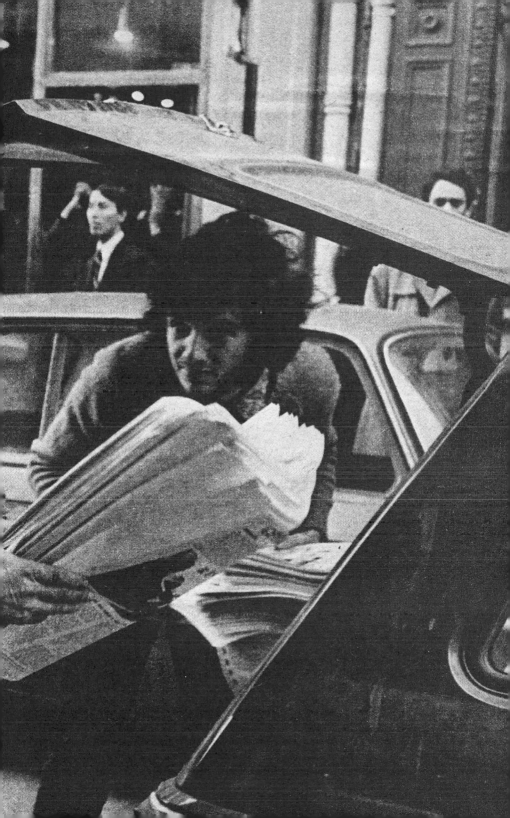

Sartre and Simone de Beauvoir during their arrest for distributing LA CAUSE DU PEUPLE *and afterwards in a police car on the way to the police station, 1971*

exception that proves the rule. As for me, I think that I'm still alive because I refused it.

CONTAT *(To Sartre and Simone de Beauvoir)*: How did you help each other in your work, your writing?

SIMONE DE BEAUVOIR: Basically what we do is read and comment on what the other has written. What I mean is, I never publish anything without first having shown the manuscript to Sartre, and it's seldom he doesn't do the same with me. We show each other what we're working on, and then we talk about it together; we tend to be pretty rough on the other, often very rough. And even if at the start we resist the other's comments or criticisms, we always think about what the other has said. The fact that we're talking about the work of someone very close to us, and knowing at the same time that it's not our own, gives us both a sympathy and perspective that are, I think, very valid. And it often happens that Sartre or I will defend our original viewpoint tenaciously, but in the end it's very rare that we don't give in.

SARTRE: I think we're right, because that in fact is precisely what Flaubert wanted: a critic who could place himself in the center of the author's ideas. And that's what we've done with each other. We each know where the other is going, what we want to say or what we want to prove. We therefore can criticize each other in the context of that knowledge, place ourselves in the center of the other's ideas. . . .

ASTRUC: Has it ever happened that you were in violent disagreement?

SARTRE: Ever? All the time! *(Laughter.)*

BOST: I can attest to that. I've heard some pretty wild screaming sessions.

SIMONE DE BEAUVOIR: There were times when we were arguing so loudly that Bost, who was on his way to have lunch with us, would arrive at the door and hear such screaming that he would tiptoe away

90

without ringing, saying: "I'll come back when things have quieted down." But the truth is, there's more violence in the tone than in fact.

SARTRE: That may be, but I can remember your saying to me once: "I can see right through you. Now I understand all your tricks. From your first book on, you've been lying through your teeth all the time. . . ." *(Laughter.)*

SIMONE DE BEAUVOIR: No, I never said you lied. What I said was: "I can see your methods, your techniques." Because the initial version of *The Respectful Prostitute* was in fact very poor. You reworked it in three days and it was fine. But the fact is, we have sometimes been very tough on each other.

CONTAT: Sartre, you've gone on record as saying that in general you prefer ladies' company to that of men. Can you tell us why?

SARTRE: First of all, there's the physical element. There are of course ugly women, but I prefer those who are pretty. Then there is the fact that they're oppressed. Therefore it's seldom they'll bore you with shop talk; they tend to situate their conversations on a higher plane of sensibility. That means you can have a conversation on a café terrace with a woman and talk about the people going by. Today women's sensibilities are more interesting than men's. Men's sensibilities, it seems to me, lack finesse; they're formed by politics and a certain number of moral principles. Man is a conventional creature. And you know what Lacan used to say: "Man is comical." Well, I think that we're all comical. And women aren't.

GORZ: Do you know, or have you had occasion to spend some time with, what is generally referred to as the "liberated" woman? The United States is filled with them.

91

SARTRE: Listen, I don't know how you think of Simone de Beauvoir, but she seems to me to be liberated enough. *(Laughter.)*.

GORZ: But you and Simone de Beauvoir don't often sit at a café terrace, I would surmise, watching the world go by or commenting on the passers-by.

SARTRE: Oh, we do, we do. We'll soon be going to lunch together, and we're going to watch the passers-by, and have a few things to say about them. We've been doing it for almost fifty years.

And I'll tell you something else: I enjoy being with a woman because I'm bored out of my mind when I have to converse in the realm of ideas.

CONTAT: Do you think that when two philosophers meet they don't have much to say to each other?

SARTRE: They are at their very worst. No question about it. *(Laughter.)*

POUILLON: As they should be!

CONTAT: Could you tell us about your meeting with Lukács, which illustrates this point rather tellingly?

SARTRE: Yes. It was at the Congress of . . . not Vienna. It was at the Congress of . . .

SIMONE DE BEAUVOIR: It was in Helsinki.

SARTRE: That's right, Helsinki. And this is more or less the exchange that took place between two sessions:

"I don't agree with you about your philosophy," Lukács said to me.

"O.K.," I said.

"You talk about people," he said. "Let's assume that these people live at a certain time."

"O.K.," I said.

"That means that they wear the clothes of the period in which they live, and eat the food of the time, right?" he said.

"Certainly," I said.

92

"And doesn't that also mean that they share the ideas of the time?" he said.

"Oh, yes," I said, "I couldn't agree more."

"Then you see," he said, "they are *of* their time."

"Yes indeed," I said, at which point the conversation broke off because the next session was about to start.

I can carry that one step further and say that I don't think I ever remember having any discussions that were useful to me. The most extended conversations I ever remember having were with Raymond Aron, when I was twenty-five. We argued and argued till we were blue in the face, he trying to pin me down or catch me out, which he was often able to do, since he was a formidable dialectician. But those arguments didn't give me anything; it was classical idealism. He was trying to corner someone who didn't have a really clear idea what he thought at that juncture of his life—it preceded *Being and Nothingness*. And with Aron I had countless arguments and discussions, but not many with other people. In the main, I tend to be a good listener, and I am interested in what other people have to say. But I don't like to argue. Discussions or arguments don't represent real relationships between people: real relationships are when you act in concert, when you decide to do something together—it may be an intellectual act, of course, such as signing some paper or writing an article—but that's the level where one can act.

Shots of Fidel Castro's arrival in Havana, in January 1959.

GORZ: Broadly speaking, *Critique de la raison dialectique* sets forth the theoretical bases for the political line that advocates mass revolutionary democracy and rejects all forms of organization,

93

control mechanisms, and management apparatuses as being deviations from the collective liberation currently underway. It considers that these structures, already ineffective and institutionalized, will be used against the proponents of the collective praxis. One could therefore say that this book is prophetic, and yet the fact remains that you discovered its salient elements in the realm of theoretical research.

SARTRE: Yes, that's true.

GORZ: When you went to Cuba in 1960, after having published *Critique de la raison dialectique*, it must have been pretty clear to you that the fragile structure of Cuba—with its serious lack of consumer goods, the blockade, and the constant threat of attack from the outside, in other words a form of popular government which the force of circumstances had never allowed to organize itself from the grass-roots up and which, therefore, was structured from the top down, and in particular through the person of a charismatic leader—would at some point come tumbling down on the Cuban leaders, and that they were heading straight into terrible troubles.

SARTRE: When I was there I used to say to them: "Your time of terror is still ahead of you."

GORZ: You told them that?

SARTRE: Yes, time and again. While I was there they asked that if I wrote any articles about my visit there, I was to describe them as democrats, not as socialists. They still did not have a solid grasp on the concept of a socialist or a communist economy as it applied to their country. The articles I later wrote, which were published in *France-Soir*, were picked up and reprinted by them in Spanish, in the Cuban press, precisely because I had refrained from talking about socialism. But there was something very special about the place in those days, doubtless because the terror was still to come, a feeling of happiness and pleasure such as I have never seen. That

Photos of Sartre and Simone de Beauvoir in Cuba, with Castro, Che Guevara, et al.

94

kind of revolution which was a holiday, a celebration, was remarkable indeed. And then, suddenly, there was a grim reminder that the revolution wasn't one long holiday. The cargo ship *La Coubre*, on its way from Europe to Cuba with a hold full of weapons, blew up without warning and killed a lot of people. It was sabotage. I don't think anyone ever found out exactly how the ship was sabotaged, but it was clear that the C.I.A. was in on it. And that incident reminded me that what was going on was not completely idyllic.

GORZ: I think we can safely say that dialectical materialism in Cuba was nonetheless heading toward the inevitable bureaucratization of that revolution, whose organizational roots were not in the people themselves the way they are in, say, China.

SARTRE: Yes, that's a fair statement.

GORZ: I'd like to ask a question slightly off the immediate subject of Cuba, although it is related. What in your opinion is the right attitude to take vis-à-vis any revolution trapped in dialectical materialism; in other words, a revolution that's beginning to go sour? How should one react to such a situation?

SARTRE: My feeling is that you have to back it as long as you can, as long as it hasn't turned completely sour, even though it be at the risk of being cuckolded later, as the Communists put it. And then you have to see how things evolve: if bureaucracy really begins to take over, you have to have the same attitude toward it as you would toward any bureaucracy—be against it. There are no two ways about it. But in Cuba that problem wasn't serious, at least in the beginning.

GORZ: I see.

SARTRE: And was it fatal? I have no idea, because in Cuba there were a lot of other areas where they went wrong, for instance in agriculture. In any case, terror is always something quite complex, the result of both internal and external pressures, and the internal circumstances presuppose the existence of a great number of failings in one area or another. Very often terror is used to cover up these failings.

GORZ: The question of Cuba is inextricably bound up with the American public. There are a great many revolutionary intellectuals in the United States, many of whom share your opinions and admire you highly. Privately, they are perfectly well aware of the historical reasons, as well as the personal factors—for example, Fidel Castro's personal weaknesses, etc.—which contributed to the gradual loss of purity of the Cuban revolution. And at the same time they say: "Here we have an island blockaded and under siege, and therefore we can't voice our reservations publicly." Not all that different from the attitude of the French Communists right after World War II with respect to the Russian camps. What would you say to these people? Would you tell them that they ought to offer, openly and candidly, an historical analysis of the revolution, showing what part the use of force and personal errors play, while at the same time they ought to make it clear they support the revolution wholeheartedly? Or would you advise them differently?

SARTRE: No, I'd tell them just what you suggested. One must consider oneself solidly behind the revolution, and yet at the same time be critical of what is open to criticism. Actually, I've always thought— and this goes back to the period of the classical intellectual, although on certain levels the truth still applies—that the situation of the intellectual can be defined by two terms: fidelity and criticism. I think that faithfulness is essential: you can't leave a group whenever you feel like it, whenever you don't agree with its political policies one hundred per cent. If you belong to it, you ought to stick with it as long as you can, or at least until the situation becomes im-

96

possible. But you must always remember that the role of an intellectual is to emphasize the principles of the revolution. And if those principles are not respected, then the intellectual has a duty to speak out and say so. Fidelity and criticism. It's no easy task, I assure you, but we have to fulfill that difficult role nonetheless, as best we can.

Shots of the Vietnam war. Bombings, soldiers setting fire to villages, torturing prisoners, having themselves photographed standing over the bodies of those they've just killed.

Shots of the War Crimes Tribunal in Stockholm, organized by Bertrand Russell, with Jean-Paul Sartre presiding.

SARTRE: ''The Russell War Crimes Tribunal was born out of this dual contradictory realization: the Nuremberg Trials pointed up the necessity of creating an investigative body to look into war crimes and, if called for, to pass judgments. Today, neither governments nor the people are in a position to create such a tribunal. We are here fully cognizant that no one has commissioned or empowered us to do what we are doing. But if we have taken the initiative, it is because we realize that no one *could* empower us. Obviously, our tribunal is not an institution; nor do we mean to replace some already existing body. Our tribunal, on the contrary, is born of a general incapacity, of a void that needs to be filled, and of a world-wide appeal that thus far has been unable to make itself heard. This Tribunal deems that its legitimacy is based in large part both on its perfect impotence and on its universality.''

At Sartre's apartment.

SARTRE: It would be preferable if the people could prevent governments from declaring war, but since

97

for the moment that is not the case, the least we can do is set up a tribunal with similar powers, subject to the approval of the people. That's what we wanted to do. Our debates and discussions were secondary in importance to our prime mission, which was to give the masses something to read and judge for themselves. And then, if we had managed to garner enough influence, enough votes, our findings would have been validated. And as it happened, we did pretty well, for we did, on the basis of the evidence presented, accuse the Americans of genocide and found them guilty of the same.

Film clips from the film Vivre sous les bombes, *directed by Madeleine Riffaut and Roger Pic, showing the North Vietnamese war effort. The soundtrack is from an address Sartre made at a meeting about Vietnam.*

SARTRE: *"Today the Vietnamese people are fighting for all of us. All the democratic and progressive forces of the world must join together to bring down the arrogant, outrageous police of the world euphemistically called free. It is in Vietnam that our fate is being determined at present; it is there that we will find out whether or not any possibility exists for us to be neither exploited nor alienated, whether or not there is any possibility for the countries of the Third World to accede to and profit from economic development and technological progress, to attain freedom and dignity. It is Vietnam, by the pain and anguish it is going through today, that is showing us the way."*

At Sartre's apartment.

GORZ: You have gone on record as saying that an intellectual must always tell the truth, and when he is involved in a revolution that deviates from its goal, or begins to founder or slip into decadence, he must denounce these errors to the members of that revolu-

98

tion. We have also said that an intellectual cannot be a leader or a person invested with organizational responsibility. In your eyes, what specifically typifies an intellectual, insofar as he participates in the world and its problems, and, secondly, what factors go into the making of an intellectual?

SARTRE: On that question, as on many others, I have evolved through the years, but I do think there is a classic intellectual—I belonged to that category, and, alas, still do, at least in part—and then there is a different kind of intellectual who came into being in May 1968. In any case, I thought that the classical intellectual—he's the one we've all known: we were born, we were brought up and educated as classical intellectuals—was from the outset someone who was recruited in a sector that I'll refer to as specialized workers of practical knowledge. These are people whose profession it is to constitute technical or practical data in some way or other on the basis of scientific knowledge. They range, therefore, from those engaged in scientific research to those who apply it, such as doctors and engineers. At that point, the intellectual can be thought to be on a plane where, individually, he makes use of the specific and he makes use of it on the basis of universal concepts or applications. Thus it is, for example, that a scientist in America, who is working on the atomic bomb or on new weapons the Americans want to try out in Vietnam, is specific to the degree that he is involved in making weapons: he is making them for the Vietnam war, or more generally for American imperialism. Yet he is still universal in the sense that he is applying to these weapons a universal knowledge: it is universally true that if you put such and such a weapon in such and such a situation, such and such dangers will result.

It is, therefore, this constant contradiction between universal knowledge and its practical or

99

*Sartre and Cohn-Bendit at press conference
on the Stammheim trial of the
Baader-Meinhof group, Stuttgart 1974*

specific utilization that creates within the technician of practical knowledge a possibility of being an intellectual. He becomes an intellectual the moment he realizes this contradiction within himself—a contradiction that resembles in many respects Hegel's uneasy conscience, for in that Hegelian concept there is, too, the universal and the specific—and comes to the conclusion that he can't resolve it. That is the classic intellectual.

What that means is that he doesn't doubt himself or question himself. He knows there is within himself a contradiction, which gives him an uneasy conscience. But he thinks that his uneasy conscience gives him the opportunity to align himself with, say, the proletariat, to whom he can give advice and counsel, to whom he can reveal certain truths. He reveals these truths as an individual who is made uneasy by this universality within himself, or as a universal being who is upset by his individuality. He suggests to the proletariat certain policies, reveals truths that are increasingly universal to his mind, and thus he sets himself up as an intellectual. What that means on a practical level is that in most cases he signs petitions. In other words, seeing the difference between a universal political concept and its application, and the specific political application and its corresponding concept, as used and abused by a bourgeois government, he *denounces* the specific concept, and the specific policy that the bourgeois use in the name of the universal. Such is the classic conception of the intellectual. He is therefore quite content to have an uneasy or unhappy conscience; he is *happy* to have it because it is that unhappy conscience that allows him to denounce. Therefore the intellectual—the classic intellectual—is a great denouncer.

All right, that, more or less, is the intellectual such as I saw him prior to May 1968. From that point on

100

something very special happened: the student movement that set the events of May 1968 going has made its way into the streets and has challenged a certain number of things, more specifically the whole professorial set-up, that is, the knowledge-equals-power concept that has historically dictated classroom conduct. And it also challenged the involvement of the state in cultural matters, and the fact that culture was limited, reserved for the happy few, whereas it should have been for everyone. And we realized, through all these specific challenges, that what they were attacking, among other things, was the classical intellectual. They criticized a whole host of things, but their real target was the classical intellectual.

And at that point one had two choices: either you got mad and you said: "Dammit! They're questioning our validity; they don't have any right to do that! What about our well-known uneasy consciences that we have by appointment from the powers-that-be? If they persist, we have no choice but to take sides against them." There was, therefore, together with the student challenges, something rotten in the realm of the classical intellectual. This is how the people who challenged and questioned the classical structure view professors: as a technician of practical knowledge, a professor in a university possesses a certain knowledge that bourgeois society had provided him with, and that knowledge is in part universal and in part specific; and as the possessor of that knowledge, he has a power, a very specific power, which is to eliminate students. An intellectual who does this is an intellectual who is not simply someone who denounces through words and who serves through words; no, he is someone who denounces through words and who, being who he is, is entrusted by bourgeois society with a bourgeois power of selection. If, consequently, these teachers want to

101

proceed in liaison with their students, if they want to remain faithful to their tendency toward universalism, they must learn to question themselves, the uneasy conscience has to go. In other words, they have to look for a new way of being with the masses, by turning their backs on whatever specific power they may have, and by accepting the same degree of sovereignty as any member of the masses, and not one iota more.

At which point you might wonder: what then makes him an intellectual, since he's integrated into the masses? And actually I suspect that in a socialist society such as we envisage it there will no longer be any intellectuals, for the very reason that the existing contradictions will be no more. At present, those among the intellectuals who have understood what I'm saying are with the masses; the only distinction is that when the occasion demands they can offer the masses, that is, the concrete universal, a tendency toward universality which is theirs because of their studies. It is still possible for the intellectual to serve the masses by giving them what they may need, since it is he, the intellectual, who possesses it. This is the prime principle of the new intellectual. It presupposes—and this is happening more and more often—an integration on the part of the intellectual in that he go work in a factory, that he give up his studies in order to become a worker among other workers. There will still remain an aura of the intellectual about him, a certain awareness or knowledge of the things he has studied, a universalism that he can place at the disposal of the masses if he wishes, but nothing more.

The Communists have never accepted the real conjunction between intellectuals and the people. They have never allowed the intellectual to immerse himself in the people so that his old persona can be dissolved. To my mind that is a very serious error.

They have left on one side an elite they refer to as intellectuals, and on the other side you have the mass of people, whereas in reality there are no masses and no elite, all there is is a totality of people who want certain things. And these people are in a certain sense alike, because what the intellectual wants, more or less, is what the mass wants. The only difference may well be that the former has the means of specifying, of putting into precise language, what the mass wants. The intellectual must follow; he must understand what the contradictions of the masses are, or what their desires are, and he must follow them without exception.

CONTAT: What did the changes that occurred in you after May 1968 bring into your life? When all is said and done, you still go on writing . . .

SARTRE: All right, if you want to carry things to this extreme, I'll be modest now, and leave the universal to focus on the specific.

POUILLON: Good. And I think it will bring us around full circle, because just now, when you were giving us your definition of the intellectual, you said he was the ''technician of practical knowledge.'' Don't you think that definition is a trifle narrow? Simply take yourself as an example: can you qualify yourself, when you were writing, say, *Nausea*, or *The Devil and the Good Lord*, as a technician of practical knowledge?

Photos of Sartre in various professorial stances.

SARTRE: No, but I was when I used to be a philosophy professor. I was a man whom bourgeois society had entrusted with transmitting cultural values.

And there's the rub as far as bourgeois society is concerned, for those intellectuals who do integrate themselves with the masses and who do take their part appear to the bourgeois as traitors. Why? Because they have taken knowledge with which they had been inculcated for a whole other purpose and used it for the wrong ends. Furthermore, some lin-

103

gering vestiges of the philosophy professor must still be with me, and that's what I have to rid myself of. I think I'm almost there, but the fact remains that I do still write books written by an intellectual, by a technician of practical knowledge.

For instance, at the same time I was discovering this new sense of who and what the intellectual is, I was also writing my *Flaubert*, which I've been working on for so many years now that I'll never abandon it. I'll finish it because it would be absurd not to, and considering that, independent of its own intrinsic value, this kind of book may be of some use to the masses. One never knows what the culture that comes after us will turn out to be. And then there is, as I have said before, the ideological interest: it's there, and has to be completed. This said, there is another reason. If I were forty or forty-five, I might well have abandoned the work. But the fact is I'm in my late sixties. And no one wants me to do my stint on the assembly line; I'd be sent back out to pasture the day I arrived. As a result, my case is rather to be, roughly speaking, a classical intellectual, and to see what the intellectual will be, what he is in the process of becoming.

SARTRE: "You're the ones who have to decide whether what Geismar did was good or bad. I want to take to the streets because I'm an intellectual and because I think that the rapport between the people and intellectuals which used to exist in the nineteenth century, not always but at that period, produced very

*Alain Geismar, a leader of the French student movement who gained prominence during and after the events of May, 1968.

104

good results. And we ought to try and re-create that rapport today.

"Fifty years ago the people and intellectuals came to a parting of the ways; now, we have to bridge that gap and bring them back together. Not so that the intellectuals can give the people advice, or tell them what to do, but on the contrary to help the masses take on a new shape. And that is why I say to you: we will find each other once again, as surely as night follows day."

The People's Tribunal in Lens, 1970. (Clips from the collective film entitled The Miners.)

A MINER: "Why do we accuse the coal companies? Because the mines are killing us more and more frequently. The Fouquières catastrophe, which we intend to pass judgment on today, is still all too fresh in our minds.

"The accusation will consist of three counts, and all three are indissolubly joined together, for the explanations offered us by the coal companies are not at all satisfactory. That is why we felt we had to constitute this people's trial."

SARTRE: "What we have to try and determine is whether the catastrophe is due to 'fate,' as the term 'accident' employed in the coal company's report suggests, or whether it was murder.

"You can if you like call 'pit gas' and 'silicosis' fatalities, but if so then they are fatalities that certain men are prey to because other men exploit them and sacrifice not only health but life on the altar of productivity.

"Between safety and profit, a choice has to be made. And in every capitalist society the choice is made ahead of time: maximum profit, therefore no safety.

"The accident could have happened anywhere. All it took was the right conditions of pit gas and

105

lack of safety measures. But these deaths were calculated. They were figured in on the annual balance sheet, the balance sheet which represents the triumph of productivity over safety.

"These deaths were known ahead of time, in those big offices where people look upon workers as simple machines, to be used until they wear out.

"I therefore suggest to you the following conclusions: The bosses' state is guilty of murder committed on February 4, 1970. The engineers in charge of Pit Number six are its executioners. Therefore, we find them also guilty of first-degree murder. First-degree because they opt for productivity over safety; that is, they judge the production of material goods more important than human lives."

Sartre conducting an investigation regarding the murder of Pierre Overney, in February 1972, in front of the Renault Auto Works.

SARTRE: "First of all, I want to find out whether private guards are armed. Who is armed? That's what we want to know."

A WORKER: "As a matter of fact, it was a cop in civvies."

SARTRE: "A cop out of uniform? Are they armed?"

A WORKER: "They are cops out of uniform. I don't know whether management knows it or not, but I find it inadmissible for a cop to be armed."

SARTRE: "Before, there was nothing like that?"

A WORKER: "No, never. On paydays there were guards around, but they were all in uniform, with their submachine guns, and that was all."

SARTRE: "Didn't anyone see the revolver? *(To a journalist.)* It looks as though a French citizen is not allowed to protest the murder of a fellow citizen by armed police at the very gates of a factory, nor is he allowed to try and get to the bottom of the crime. If that is allowed to happen, then things are at a sorry

106

pass; there is a growing wave of violence that at some point is going to explode. We have to get to the root of the matter and find out what really happened.''

A JOURNALIST: ''Do you feel you have to carry out your own investigation? Don't you have any confidence in the established authorities?''

SARTRE: ''No, none at all.''

A JOURNALIST: ''And what do you think of the Communist Party's attitude?''

SARTRE: ''It's absurd. They say to you: 'The proof that they* are in cahoots is that they're killing each other off.' That argument doesn't make much sense. And it looks to me as though it's the Communists who are in cahoots with the government, against the Maoists.''

At Sartre's apartment.

SARTRE: Fascism as we've known it in the past was characterized by certain traits, namely the existence of leaders, both military and civilian, with dictatorial powers, who were supported by a large political party. And this Fascist Party acted as an intermediary between the dictators and the people, whom it oppressed and brutalized rather than consulted. And I thought, therefore, that since in France there wasn't any powerful party, we could not be heading toward Fascism. But for some time I've been thinking that the major party that seemed to be missing, the party that would serve the dictators, might well be the Communist Party itself. In other words, if the Communist Party is thought of as the Fascist Party, mediating between the masses to whom it does not give the truth but whom it terrorized to a degree—as

*That is, the bourgeois and the Maoists

it did in proclaiming that the proof the Maoists and the bourgeois were working together was in Pierre Overney's murder, which is the most stupid notion I've ever heard—then there you have the missing link. And the way its thinking is going these days, it will end up as the intermediary we mentioned, and will therefore have all the elements characteristic of Fascism.

Shots of Pierre Overney's funeral. Marchers from the Place de la Republique to the Pere-Lachaise Cemetery.

NARRATOR: *"The funeral took place in February 1972. Never, since May of 1968, had the Revolutionary New Left assembled so many people in the streets of Paris. But, with Pierre Overney's funeral, the various elements of the Left reached a momentary high point. The ebb was quick to come: the traditional left wing organized the electoral strategy of a Common Program. As for the Maoists, they decided to dissolve their organization.*

"Sartre, together with his comrades, pursued the search for a socialism without any previous model, without authority, without delegation of power: a libertarian socialism.

"In 1973, a new project befell him, that of the daily newspaper Liberation, *which undertook the difficult task of trying to survive without initial capitalization, without any support, and without advertising: a journal of popular opinion. Today that effort is well on its way to succeeding, and Sartre still remains affiliated with the paper, although illness has forced him to give up his duties as editor-in-chief.*

"Another project had to be abandoned: the fourth volume of Flaubert. *Due to an illness that affected his eyesight, Sartre has had to give up all thought of ever completing that monumental work. In fact, he is currently forbidden to either read or write.*

108

"When that happened, he threw himself heart and soul into a plan for a number of television programs in which he would present the first seventy-five years of this century. These programs will not be made. The Powers-that-Be have so decreed. The liberalism of the Giscard administration doubtless fears the possible repercussions, and the effects on the average Frenchman, that these programs on the history of our era as seen by the philosopher of freedom, Jean-Paul Sartre, may have.

Music: A Beethoven Quartet.

"Still in all, Sartre goes on. At the present time, he is hard at work, with the help of his friend Pierre Victor, on a new manuscript, the title of which is Power and Freedom."

FILM CREDITS

The National Audio-Visual Institute
Presents

SARTRE
BY HIMSELF

Produced by:

PIERRE-ANDRE BOUTANG
GUY SELIGMANN

Directed by:

ALEXANDRE ASTRUC
MICHEL CONTAT

Editing:	ANNIE CHEVALLY
Director of Photography:	RENATO BERTA
Sounds Effects:	LUC PERINI
Sound Technicians:	ANTONIO GRIGIONI
	ALAIN SEMPE
Research Assistant:	MICHELE FOURNIER

We wish to thank the following people for their collaboration on the interviews:

SIMONE DE BEAUVOIR
JACQUES-LAURENT BOST
ANDRE GORZ
MARIE OLIVIER
FRANCOIS PERIER
JEAN POUILLON
SERGE REGGIANI

Music:

BEETHOVEN
WEBERN
(interpreted by the
Fontanarosa Quartet)

With the voices of:

JACQUES FRANTZ
SERGE REGGIANI
FRANCOISE GIRET
PHILIPPE ADRIEN

Thanks too to the following who helped make the film possible:

ROBERT ALAZRAKI
CHRISTIAN BAILLEMONT
ROLAND BERNARD
PIERRE BEUCHOT
JEAN-FRANCOIS CASI
CYRIL CHARDON
SOPHIE CLAVEL
EMMANUEL CLOT
HENRI CZAP
GHISLAINE GODLEWSKY
HENRI JOLY

111

ETINNE JOURDAN
PIERRE LENOIR
EMMANUEL MACHUEL
LOUISETTE NEIL
JACQUES PAMART
JEAN-PIERRE PLATEL
FRANCOISE RENY
JEAN-FRANCOIS ROBIN
HENRI ROSSIER
PATRICE ROYER
CLAUDE SICHERE
NOEL VERY
CAROLE VIAN
ROGER VINGEL
MONIQUE VILLECHENOUX

This film was a production of the National Audiovisual Institute in Paris, and the Sodaperaga Company, also of Paris.

OTHER BOOKS OF INTEREST PUBLISHED BY URIZEN

LITERATURE

Bataille, Georges
Story of the Eye,
120 p. / Cloth $5.95

Bresson, Robert
Notes on Cinematography,
132 p. / $6.95 / paper $3.50

Brodsky, Michael
Detour, novel,
350 p. / Cloth $8.95

Cohen, Marvin
The Inconvenience of Living, fiction,
200 p. / Cloth $8.95 / paper $4.95

Ehrenburg, Ilya
The Life of the Automobile, novel,
192 p. / Cloth $8.95 / paper $4.95

Enzensberger, Hans Magnus
Mausoleum, poetry,
132 p. / Cloth $10.00 / paper $4.95

Hamburger, Michael
German Poetry 1910-1975,
576 p. / Cloth $17.50 / paper $7.95

Handke, Peter
Nonsense & Happiness, poetry,
80 p. / Cloth $7.95 / paper $3.95

Innerhofer, Franz
Beautiful Days, novel,
228 p. / Cloth $8.95 / paper $4.95

Kroetz, Franz Xavier
Farmyard & Other Plays,
192 p. / Cloth $12.95 / paper $4.95

Shepard, Sam
*Angel City, Curse of the Starving
    Class & Other Plays,*
300 p. / Cloth $15.00 / paper $4.95

MOLE EDITIONS

Clastres, Pierre
Society Against the State,
188 p. / Cloth $12.95

Elias, Norbert
The Civilizing Process, Vol. 1 & 2,
400 p. / Cloth $15.00 each Vol.

Gibson, Ian
The English Vice,
364 p. / Cloth $12.95

Schivelbusch, Wolfgang
The Railway Journey,
275 p. / photos / Cloth $15.00 ·

Sternberger, Dolf
Preface by Erich Heller
Panorama of the 19th Century
212 p. / Cloth $15.00

ECONOMICS

DeBrunhoff, Suzanne
Marx on Money,
192 p. / Cloth $10.00 / paper $4.95

Howard, Dick
The Marxian Legacy,
340 p. / Cloth $15.00 / paper $5.95

Linder, Marc
Anti-Samuelson, Vol. I,
400 p. / Cloth $15.00 / paper $5.95
Anti-Samuelson, Vol. II,
440 p. / Cloth $15.00 / paper $5.95

CONTEMPORARY AFFAIRS

Andrew Arato / Eike Gebhardt (Eds.)
*The Essential Frankfurt School
    Reader,*
554 p. / Cloth $17.50 / paper $6.95

Augstein, Rudolf
Preface by Gore Vidal
Jesus, Son of Man,
420 p. / Cloth $12.95 / paper $4.95

Burchett, Wilfred
Southern Africa Stands Up,
Cloth 12.95 / paper $4.95

Kristeva, Julia
About Chinese Women,
250 p. / Cloth $8.95

Ledda, Galvino
Padre, Padrone,
Cloth $9.95

Sartre, Jean-Paul
Sartre by Himself,
136 p. / photos / Cloth $10.95 / paper $3.95

Steele, Jonathan
Inside East Germany,
300 p. / Cloth $12.95

Stern, August
The USSR vs. Dr. Mikhail Stern,
420 p. / Cloth $12.95

Write for a complete catalog and send orders to:
Urizen Books, Inc., 66 West Broadway, New York, N.Y. 10007
212 · 962-3413